A CLASS OF OUR OWN

A CLASS OF OUR OWN

Conversations about class in Ireland

Edited by
Patrick O'Dea

Dublin

A Class of our Own
is first published in 1994 by
New Island Books
2, Brookside,
Dundrum Road,
Dublin 14,
Ireland.

ISBN 1 874597 02 2

New Island Books receives financial assistance from
The Arts Council (An Chomhairle Ealaíon),
Dublin, Ireland.

Cover design by Jon Berkeley.
Typeset by Graphic Resources.
Printed in Ireland by Colour Books Ltd., Baldoyle.

Contents

A CLASS OF OUR OWN

Do mo bhean, Meabh

EDITOR'S NOTE

In 1992 eleven Irish men and women sat in front of a tape recorder to address a subject which is rarely openly discussed in Ireland. They answered questions about their awareness of social class (or lack of it) during their early years, their contacts with people from social classes other than their own, their changes in status (and/or perceptions) as they grew older, and their feelings about the issue of social class at the present time.

The transcripts of their replies have been edited and, in some cases, shortened to avoid repetitions. Despite these minor editorial interventions, the words of each speaker have been carefully preserved, and his (or her) tone of voice — and accent, emphasis and turn of phrase — can hopefully be heard as one reads through each chapter.

If there is an emphasis on one class, then it is the middle class experience in Ireland, as, increasingly the values, attitudes, feelings and conditioning of middle class life are accepted in society as the standard to which Irish people should either live or aspire to live.

For Joseph O'Connor being middle class is "knowing the day would not come when the bailiffs would arrive". It is an insulation from the rough edges of life. "It is security, encouragement, comfort and a nice sense of excitement from time to time." (Frances Fitzgerald). However, for Peter McVerry "the middle-class is a ghetto, as much as Sherriff street is a ghetto... middle class people... are trapped within a very narrow range of views, of attitudes, and even of values, many of which they might be unaware of..."

It is with Peter McVerry, a Jesuit talking of his voluntary engagement with the poor in an inner-city area, that the book opens. Part One reflects the experience of three men from working-class Dublin backgrounds; the interviews in Part Two — the core of the collection — constitute a virtual self-portrait of middle-class Ireland; while Part Three provides the sole

11

contribution from what might be termed the country's upper-class (or aristocracy). Dr. Noel Browne concludes with a moving account of his childhood and the efforts he has made, throughout his life, to combat some of the evils brought about by the class system. His experience ranges widely over every level of social class in Ireland; and his opinions challenge our complacencies.

All these interviews are not in the realm of censored mediated thought or public performance. Interviewees talk, with whatever ease or unease they have, around the topic of how social class was for them. The interviews are not for judgement, they are for listening to. It has been said that in England there is a class system and nobody talks about it, in America there is no such thing as a class system and everybody talks about it, and in Ireland there is a class system but nobody is quite sure what it is. Perhaps the interviews in this book may start to provide some clues to that puzzle.

Patrick O'Dea,
Dublin,
1994.

PROFESSOR ANTHONY CLARE

Foreword

It is a brave person who attempts to make generalisations about class, to unravel assumptions about class, to challenge stereo types. There is a complex and diverse academic literature concerning class, but wisely Patrick O'Dea has eschewed the ideal of adding to it. Instead he has chosen to talk to a sample of contemporary Irish people who, like him, share an interest in the way that their psychological and social consciousness have been shaped by class factors. It is obviously not a representative sample — no random selection is at work, no compensation for religion, gender or occupational status, no attempt to obtain a reasonable cross-section in terms of age. It is a subjective, personal, introspective reflection on the role of class in Irish life and is none the worse for that.

From the outset, though, class remains a difficult issue to define, particularly in Ireland. There has never been a substantial industrialised proletariat. Aside from the Anglo-Irish ascendancy of the Big House, represented here by Lord Inchiquin, (and he is quick to point out that his was not a particularly affluent upbringing and that looking after property without the financial wherewithal engenders ulcers not happiness) there has never been a particularly identifiable and influential Irish upper class. Rather Irish social divisions have been rural and urban, "culchie" and "jackeen", professional and trade, owner/occupier and renter, moneyed and impoverished, educated and unschooled. The most striking class divide is identifiable when all the positive and all the negative elements come together — the university educated, home owning, Dublin professional on the one hand, the farm hand who leaves school at 14 and lives in a rented cottage on the other. The powerful picture painted by Noel Browne of his mother dying in poverty — a memory that, as he sadly observes all these years later, overshadowed his life forever — embodies this division between "the haves and the have- nots" ordained, as he sarcastically notes, by the Will or God and His Holy Mother. The Irish middle class were once defined as "working class people who don't know it". But perhaps they do know it, which is why so many of them vociferously insist on their middle-classness, frightened by Noel Browne's haunting vision "of the possibility of poverty" and the humiliations endured by the truly impoverished in our midst.

For all the insistence on the lack of wide class disparities, there is a remarkable consensus amongst the contributors that there is a recognisable class system in Ireland and it is rigidly maintained. Yet few portray middle-classness as a particularly attractive option. To Fr. Peter McVerry it is a ghetto as much as Sherriff Street is a ghetto in which people remain trapped within a narrow range of attitudes, views, values even. Indeed his is a devastating, challenging contribution. The poor, in his view, are quite simply the privileged. His personal transformation occurred not as a result of reading about them in his privileged middle-class setting but by encountering them in an unforgettable way in the slums of Summerhill. "I began to see life as people at the bottom see it." He insists that his middle classness is a "barrier" that will separate him for the rest of his life from the poor, and this notion of the impenetrable barriers of class is echoed by Carmencita Hederman describing the lack of contacts outside the family structure in her own reasonably-secure middle-class upbringing and echoed again in Finbarr Flood's description of people's amazement when they realise that someone with a strong Dublin accent can hold a top administrative position. Lord Inchiquin too is trapped by that self-same marker of class, namely accent — he plaintively mourns the fact that he is automatically assumed to be English and upper class because he speaks with an English accent whereas, as everyone should know, he is one of the 19 Irish Chiefs! Class is indeed a box in which fate places you and however much you move, you never leave the box. But Mick Rafferty wonders whether the real weakness is the refusal of many people to be socially mobile and the preference for the comforting reassurance of your own group.

The institution of the family is often portrayed as elementally middle class and several of the contributors subscribe to such a view. Joe O'Connor, Joe Duffy and Noel Browne express in varying ways critical views concerning the narrowness, selfishness, smugness of family life — "amoral familism" is Browne's view, yet the self-same institution viewed through the eyes of Alice Taylor or Mick Doyle or Frances Fitzgerald takes on a rosier, warmer, seductive glow — reflecting the truth that when people talk in detached, abstract, lofty terms about aspects of the human condition they are so often talking revealingly about themselves.

There is more of a consensus in this collection about the relative lack of wealth when the contributors were growing up — even the best off were by today's standards not all that different from those not quite as fortunate. Frances Fitzgerald, Mick Doyle, Joe O'Connor, Finbarr Flood, while all from different backgrounds, provide the same message; Ireland of thirty, forty, fifty years ago seemed a more homogeneous place. And then there is Noel Browne's disturbing recollection to set against such reassurance!

The problem — and it is illustrated by these absorbing recollections — is that what we know of class reflects what we ourselves have experienced; the rest, as Fr. McVerry points out in his rather unsettling way, is book theory. Many of the contributors wonder whether there was much unemployment when they were growing up, for they don't recall seeing any. My own wife's grandmother argued furiously that James Joyce was wrong in portraying Nightown in Ulysses because there were no poor in Dublin. What she meant was she never saw any. And therein lies yet again the main problem with class — it insulates us all in boxes. It is difficult to know how the other half lives for all the chat about global villages and the revelatory impact of television. There are still people who seriously doubt that there is "real" poverty in Dublin or that the impact of unemployment is psychologically and socially devastating, not because they are unintelligent — because they are not — but because they do not see these consequences and if you cannot see something, it must not be there.

This book makes its own contribution. No barrier will be broken, but unease concerning the psychological and social impact and consequences of barriers of class may be spread and at least some of the contributors and certainly the editor will be pleased! Turn off the television and talk to each other, Alice Taylor declares at one stage, as she laments the loss of community and the sense of belonging in today's world where we know more about what happens in New York than on our street. Turn off the television and read this book would be my suggestion, and learn a little about life and longing in contemporary Ireland through a handful of people who have taken a little time and trouble to think about both, and in the process have learned a little about themselves and the rest of us.

PETER McVERRY

The Summerhill Option

Peter McVerry was born in Belfast in 1944, and grew up in Newry where he attended the local Christian Brothers Primary School. At the age of twelve he went to Clongowes Wood College, and in 1962 he joined the Jesuits and studied philosophy and theology at Milltown Park, Dublin. He taught for two years in Belvedere College before being ordained in 1975. In 1974 he went to live and work in Summerhill in the inner city where he got involved in youth work. As a result of his experience there, he started a small community-based hostel for homeless boys in the inner city which he ran until 1980. He then transferred to Ballymun where he now lives. He works in the Jesuit Centre for Faith and Justice and runs several hostels for homeless boys in Dublin.

It happened quite by chance. I was teaching in Belvedere as a scholastic when somebody invited me to work in a youth club in the inner city. My involvement in the youth club became greater and greater, and eventually became all-absorbing. An opportunity arose in 1974 to live and work full-time in the inner city and because of my experience of the youth club I felt this was something I would like to do. It was only at a much later stage that I reflected back and said this was what God wanted me to do. What God wants any of us to do is to make an option for the poor in our own different ways. At that point it became a clear choice that this was where I wanted to work, to continue working for the rest of my life. If circumstances were different I could now be teaching very well-off kids, without questioning what I was doing, or without realising that I had missed something exciting and important. I had been given an opportunity.

Belvedere or Ballymun

As a Jesuit, my thinking would have been the general thinking of a religious person in the early seventies. I was available to my order and to my superiors to do whatever they felt was needed. It wasn't up to me to make the choice. So working with the poor or teaching in a well-to-do college were equal choices. I suppose I was consciously testing the waters, and finding out where I would like to work, where I would be happy working. Apart from working in the youth club I was teaching in Belvedere. I also taught in Kevin Street College of Technology. I had started a Ph.D in UCD and taught there as well. But the ultimate choice was with my superiors, and whatever they said I would do.

Nowadays I would be much clearer in making an option for the poor. It is a demand made on all of us by God. It is my personal desire now, the priority in my life. It is a commitment to those who are poor, a commitment that no matter what job I might be given by my religious order, my concern in that job would be to try to work with the poor. Even if I were now sent to teach the well-to-do, in a well-to-do college, my concern would be to use the opportunities there to help the poor, either directly in my spare time, or by being subversive and trying to change the whole structure and rationale at the college to make it less elitist and open to everybody. That is the way I now believe I have given my life to God in the Society of Jesus, and to do something that I consider worthwhile. The most worthwhile task for me is trying to achieve a better society and that is the reason why I am happy to continue giving my life to God in the Society. There is no other reason for making the sacrifices one makes as a priest.

Choose Johnny or Jilly

Prior to actually working fulltime in the inner City, my attitude to life was that God loves everybody and wants to help. So here I am. It was for my superiors, who presumably had an overview, to decide where exactly and in what way exactly I was going to help. At that time the view was that everybody was equal, everybody was equally loved by God; it didn't really matter whether you helped Johnny or Jilly, it didn't matter what social group or what income bracket they belonged to or what problems they had. Everybody needed help, and you helped whoever you could.

Now my experiences would allow me to see things very differently. Those who are poor are a privileged group in God's eyes and they are the ones for whom we make an option — everybody is not equal in that sense. We make an option for those who are less privileged in society and our primary aim is to help them, to help them, above all, to help themselves. I am therefore no longer indifferent as to whether I ought to be sent to help Johnny or Jilly. I would make choices now as to whether I should be helping Johnny or Jilly. Not that Johnny or Jilly don't both need help, but priorities need to be made. And the choice must always favour those who are poor and marginalised in society. That is the priority, it seems to me, that the gospel is demanding of us. It is also the priority that my own experience has led me to make. When I first went to live in Summerhill in the inner city it was a real eye-opener. I really began to see the suffering of people there, most of it totally unnecessary; through appalling housing, through lack of educational resources, through discrimination, through harassment by police. The way these people are treated by so many groups in society simply appals me. It is so unnecessary: it has to be changed. Working for and with these people became far more important to me than working for and with any other group.

Moving-in With The Poor

Locating myself with the poor involved re-organisation of life and attitude. Life became more simple. Anything I had materially was robbed, so I learned not to have anything of much value or I just got used to replacing things at regular intervals.

I gave up a lot of privacy. I haven't had my own room for years. I share a room with another Jesuit during most of the day or with a youth club. My bedroom at the moment is in the hostel and is shared with four kids. Giving up a place you can call your own is perhaps the most difficult thing, although I didn't find it particularly difficult.

The change of attitude was total. My assumptions and values were challenged, even the theology I had been taught. I began to see life as people at the bottom of society see it. For example, I always believed that the police were there to help, were on your side. Then I began to see that people were, in some cases, appallingly treated, and I began to ask what is going on here? Who are the good guys? And who are the bad guys?

Things were not as cut and dried as I had thought. I was shocked at the way society looked on these kids whom I was trying to help, and their families. They were extremely fine people, struggling hard to survive very difficult circumstances. They were treated as dirt, as dogs, as no good, as scum. There were letters to the papers that they should all be locked up and the keys thrown away — insulting remarks and attitudes poured out on good people. I began to ask where are the Christian values in this? I was finding far more Christianity in the people I was working with than in the more respectable areas of society, so free with their comments and attitudes. I began a total process of questioning: what is going on in our society? Questioning along these lines certainly complicated my thinking. Things were comfortable in black and white, nice simple categories that I had thought in up to then were shattered and I had to stop thinking in categories, I had to stop thinking in generalisations. I had to learn to say: here is a kid and he robs, but there is an awful lot of good in him; here is a man who is respectable, has made a lot of money, there is an awful lot of bad in him. In the balance there might not be an awful lot of difference between the two. Yet one is treated by society in a particular way and the other is treated by society in a totally different way.

Ministering on the Wrong Side of the Tracks

I think perhaps the difficulties are over-acknowledged. I mean, people come up to me and say, "God I think it's marvellous you're living there in Ballymun", or "you are living there in Summerhill, I don't know how you do it. It must be really tough for you, but you're looking well on it, you know". And I sort of scratch my head because I don't find it tough at all, certainly not now. I don't think I ever really did. I enjoy it. I would find it much tougher to go and live in a big Jesuit institution and teach all day long. People have this image that it is an awful lot tougher than it actually is.

We Have it so Easy

We don't experience life in Ballymun the way a family has to experience it; we don't have kids growing up. For a family in Ballymun, there are often worries about things like, is my kid going to start taking drugs? When are the police going to knock on my door to say Johnny has been arrested? If they really can't take it anymore; if Ballymun really gets to them and they are really depressed, there is nothing they can do about it. If I get depressed in Ballymun, my provincial has me out and over in Milltown the next day because I'm no good to him if I'm depressed. If I get sick, my provincial has me in the Mater Private Hospital. He has to, because I am no good to him on a sick bed. Whereas somebody in Ballymun, maybe a family, if they get seriously ill they may have to wait for a year for that operation. The pressures of living in Ballymun are not nearly as great for us as they are for people who are actually living there, who are growing up there and who have no choice about it because they are there for life. We are doing it voluntarily, we can stop doing it anytime we want to, and that makes a huge difference.

I have always said, we can go and we can live with people who are poor, but we can't live like them because we cannot experience what it is like to be in Ballymun, to be unable to get out of

21

Ballymun, to be sick in Ballymun, to bring up kids in Ballymun, to be unemployed in Ballymun. We don't have those experiences and that is where the difficulties of life are for most of the people in Ballymun. By contrast we have it easy.

My contacts now with the middle class are very few. In fact, most of my time is spent with people who are much poorer. I can't ever remember discussing what it means to be middle class with anybody who is middle class. I really don't have any interest in the middle class.

Being Middle-Class is a Barrier

I am personally middle class and that is a barrier that will remain for the rest of my life, from people who are poor. It certainly conditions you; it conditions your way of thinking, and one of the primary reasons for going to live in a poorer area is not that I can help the poor, but that I can be educated. You go there to learn, you go there to receive, not to live, because in order to really make this option for the poor you have got to unlearn all that conditioning, all those middle-class values, attitudes, assumptions. They all have to be unlearned and upturned, uprooted as it were. It takes years and years of working very closely with people who are poor, before you begin to see what life is really like when you are poor and marginalised. And until you have that sort of empathy, that sort of understanding of what life is like, you are really not going to be much good to anybody, because you are coming from a totally different position. I suppose the final answer to that is that I don't have time for reflecting on being middle class. It might be useful and all that, but most people are run off their feet, working in areas like Ballymun or Summerhill. It is a bit of a luxury too, a luxury to be able to sit down and start reflecting on that.

There is a real danger of romanticizing the poor. One goes and works amongst the poor, whether it be the poor in El Salvador, or the poor in South Africa or the poor in Ballymun. The poor are like anybody else, they have terrific virtues and they have terrific vices. They can be extremely frustrating, you can feel you are going nowhere, that you are up against a wall. You get stabbed in the back, you get leaped on, and you experience a rough side of life when you are working with the poor and you can sometimes feel like, ah! what the hell is the point in the whole thing. You can feel maybe you don't want to go on, you get a lot of disappointments, a lot of frustrations, but on the other hand the people are like anyone else, when one relates to them on a one-to-one basis. There is extraordinary generosity there; extraordinary tolerance I think, and a terrific resilience that they can cope with very difficult circumstances and still go out in the evening and have a good laugh. There is a much greater togetherness amongst the poor than you get in middle-class areas. It is something that is imposed on them; if you don't have a car to go off to your friends, or to go off to entertainment in another part of the city, you are thrown back much more on what is immediately around you, and that includes your own neighbours, so that there is a greater neighbourliness, than you would get in many middle-class areas. They are people, the same as rich people, and basically they have many very good qualities and they have many that aren't so good. They could say the same about me.

Growing up in Newry

I grew up in Newry, a small provincial town. My father was a doctor, so we lived in a fairly well-to-do area of the town. Our friends were pretty middle-class, and being from Newry, my primary concept of the difference between people, was religious or political. It was Catholics versus Protestants.

I remember the first time I got to know somebody very well; I was only about eight or nine. I palled around with him for a few months, and then I discovered that his family was Protestant. I was sort of shocked and wondered if I should continue palling around with him. That was the primary social division growing up in the North of Ireland.

I was aware, because my father was a doctor, that there were poor areas in Newry, but I didn't know anything about them and I had no contact with them. Basically they were just there. For a while we lived in the centre of Newry and we knew the family next door very well. We played around with the kids there. They were working-class, extremely nice people but I wasn't conscious of any great distinction. I knew my dad was a doctor and their father was a caretaker of the Town Hall. I might have been conscious that they had less money than we had, but that was all. There wasn't any consciousness of class. There were housing blocks, or local authority housing, and my memory of them is much the same as I would have of the local authority housing estates today. Houses or flats very close together in very run-down, monotonous sort of surroundings; not very well kept, obviously not a lot of care given to the environment immediately surrounding the area. I mean not an awful lot different from Sheriff Street or Darndale today.

Concerning the people living in such places, I just presumed everybody was the same, everybody lived their lives the same as I did. I presumed everybody played, some played golf, some played football, some played tennis, some cricket. I just thought everybody was equal, that people made their choices, that choices weren't imposed on people.

I suppose we picked up the attitudes of our parents, picked them up by listening and observing, rather than been told anything specifically. I suppose there was a sense that people who were poorer were inferior. You don't want to turn out like them, you don't want to end up like them. It was perhaps used like a sort of stick hanging over you, be good or you will end up like them. So I would say the attitudes were quite negative. I didn't know where they came from, or anything. In Newry everybody went to the same schools, there wasn't any social division in school, so you sat in the class and the kid beside you may have come from a very poor area in Newry but you either didn't know or you didn't care. I wasn't aware of social division, it didn't impact on me in any way. Certainly educational social division

24

was very much reduced compared to what I would now experience in Dublin.

Clongowes: Like Going Through a Tunnel

Later I went to Clongowes, and the main impact of Clongowes was again not making you aware of social class, but isolating you from the provincialism of a town like Newry. Clongowes was a very international community. You had kids from all over the world, from all sorts of backgrounds and experiences. There was a richness of experience there, and the idea of going back into living your life out in Newry just became impossible.

I lost friends once I went to boarding school. When I came home on holidays, which were pretty rare in those days — it was a few weeks at Christmas, two weeks at Easter and the summer holidays — there was no incentive to make friends amongst kids in Newry of your own age because you would be gone for the next three or four months off to boarding school. So we had a small circle of friends, who usually lived fairly locally, or who were children of close friends of our parents. That was the peer group that we associated with when we were on these rather short holidays from boarding school.

I never experienced going to Clongowes, as a class thing. Going to boarding school was like going through a tunnel, and coming out in this vast expanse, with much richer foliage and countryside to the one you had come from, and it was so much bigger, so much richer than the one you had come from. To return again to living full-time in a provincial town would have felt like you had to pull in all these parts of yourself and sort of enclose them again in a little environment that would have been very stifling.

The Doctor's Son

I suppose we were upper middle-class; a doctor in a small provincial town was a person of very high status. It wasn't a status that isolated him from other people, a doctor was seen as somebody who made a commitment of service to people and he could be called out at two o'clock in the morning to the poorest person in the area and he would go, and there wasn't the slightest problem. I think a doctor, although very middle-class, was also seen as a person at the service of the public, and a committed public servant at that.

We lived very comfortably, we lived in a very large house with a very large garden. In the early days we had pigs, I don't even know how common that was at that time. We had a car, there were not too many of them on the road. We were one of the first that had a television in the town, so we lived very comfortably, money wasn't a problem, at least never to us. We didn't get everything we wanted by any means, but we always had presents at Christmas and birthdays, certainly always enough to eat. We were allowed to go to the pictures every so often, we played in a local golf club where my father was also a member. Money didn't seem to be a problem, restricting us from doing anything, yet I think my parents were keen not to spoil us. Our standard of living was much the same as that of my pals. Most of our friends would have been in the same social grouping. Their parents were professional people, some were teachers, some were architects, one or two would have been more working-class, but we were not aware of any discrepancy in standard of living. Some might have lived in a smaller house than we did, but it wasn't an issue.

My parents would have presumed that we were going to become professional people, but that wouldn't have just been my parents. I mean everybody who did a Leaving Cert in those days automatically went on to a third level education if they wanted to. Pressure for exam results was non-existent in those days. Everybody in Clongowes would have been presumed to be going on to be a professional person. Everybody who did their Leaving Certificate had the option, provided their parents could afford to pay for university education. A pass in your Leaving Certificate automatically qualified you for a professional job, so the choice was actually made at the time at which you chose second level education. By choosing second level education with a view to doing the Leaving Certificate you were choosing a middle-class future for yourself. There was certainly no pressure put on any of us to chose a particular profession. We were free to chose what we wanted to choose.

What Does a Jesuit Do?

I suppose academic progress and sport were the two measures of success. I was fairly good at both, so I didn't have to work at trying to win extra approval, and I never experienced anything but the approval of my parents. There was never any sense that you are missing out on this; you should do better at this. I never had that experience. My parents are very happy I am doing what I want to do, but by and large they find it difficult to understand. They didn't put any obstacle in my way to becoming a Jesuit, but they did try to make sure that it was what I really wanted to do. But I never felt that they were trying to put any obstacles in my way. I think what they find difficult is when people ask what am I doing. They find it hard to give an answer. If I was teaching in Belvedere, they could say he is teaching in Belvedere and everybody knows what teaching in Belvedere means. Now they say he is working with young people. What is he doing? I am not sure what he is doing with them. He goes to court with them, and some of them are drug addicts. I am not sure what he does exactly. So they find it hard to put me into a category, or put me into a box which they can then hand to people and say: this is what he is doing. They would also be worried because to them my life is difficult, living in a poor area; and it is working with people that they would have very little knowledge or contact with. They would be a bit worried, perhaps, as to what the effect of this is having on me both materially, physically and also psychologically. They would certainly feel perhaps that I was becoming very radical compared to their views. They would be worried about my not fitting this nice standard stereotype status in society that they would imagine for a Jesuit.

Suppressed Emotions

Certainly feelings in our family were not expressed or they were expressed very infrequently or in secret as it were, except at obvious times like a death; but feelings were generally suppressed. We felt both loved by and loving towards our parents, but we weren't a family that were very expressive. We kept it to ourselves. And it was a similar situation in school; certainly at boarding school you don't express your feelings. So I would say that I have developed into a person who doesn't express his feelings. You didn't express anger, you didn't cry, you didn't express your feelings, you were kind to people, you were nice to people but you didn't actually go out hugging them or anything. There was probably a sense, too, that girls could cry, but boys couldn't.

I don't really see that there are any great advantages to a middle-class upbringing, apart from those from a personal, individual point of view, which are obviously beneficial. As money was not a problem, we were free from having to worry about the necessities of life. We were free to explore any opportunity for development that we wished to pursue, either to learn the piano or to play golf, tennis or take up any hobby or interest. On the downside you certainly learned to look at life from a very advantaged point of view, you didn't have to struggle for anything, life was relatively easy. Everything was handed to you on a plate, as it were; your position in society, your opportunities, they were all given with your social status. That is a very restricted experience, because you begin to think that life is like that for everybody, and that those who do not succeed in the way you succeed have failed through their own fault. Middle-class by it's very nature is limited, and unless something is done to help you recognise the limitations of that view, I think it can breed very unhealthy and untrue attitudes and values. We had a very uncritical attitude to life and to society. We looked up to anyone who was successful, whether it were in the political or business world, or even in the pop industry like Cliff Richards. We wouldn't have been at all critical of how they had become successful or the method they had used, or even of the whole structure of society that allowed certain people to become successful while preventing others. That understanding of what is happening in society was totally absent. We believed that those who were successful had made it because of hard work and enterprise. They were really people to be admired. Those who didn't make it, failed because they weren't prepared to work hard enough; didn't have it in them. This was where you could end up if you didn't watch yourself. We thought well of Kennedy, Lemass, De Valera. In sport it would have been Tony O'Reilly or Stanley Mathews.

A Shrinking World

I have little present-day contact with middle-class people. I know quite a number, but I see them very seldom. Unless they rang me and tied me down to a specific date, I would never get around to dropping socially into their houses and sitting down for a cup of coffee. So my world has shrunk very much and has become much more confined to poorer areas and poor people. I think that is where I find myself most comfortable. I actually find myself feeling very uncomfortable going to a middle-class home, unless I know the people very well. I can't relax and forget about the class thing. I am very conscious of it and I find it very inhibiting. I just want to get out of it as quickly as possible and get back to where I feel more at ease. My middle-class friends are people I have known for a long time; (from school, or going back many years), so we simply meet because we have known one another for so long. There is not a particular interest or issue around which we would actually meet. All my other contacts would be from a working angle; social workers, probation officers or teachers or professional people in many capacities. But it would be a working relationship rather than the development of a friendship.

Breaking Out of the Ghetto

I think that the middle class is a ghetto, as much as Sheriff Street is a ghetto. I think that middle-class people, unless they make the effort to break out, are trapped within a very narrow range of views, of attitudes, and even of values, many of which they might be unaware of; just as poor people are trapped within a certain range of ideas, and values and attitudes which they may be unaware of. I think each social class is a ghetto of it's own. To understand what is happening in society, I think each of us has to break out of our social class, to the extent that you can understand and appreciate the views, attitudes and values of people from other social classes. You don't do that without an awful lot of effort and without going outside your own social class and making friends with people. You don't get it by reading books, you don't get it by watching documentaries. You get it by living with and learning from people whose views and attitudes and values have been shaped by the experience of being poor and marginalised. I think that is one of the key issues in Irish society at the moment, and that if we are to get change, society will have to give a better deal and a fairer share of what this world has to offer to those at the bottom. That can only come about when the views and attitudes and values of the under-privileged are understood and appreciated and listened to. This will only happen when people who make the decisions in our society really know what it is like to be at the bottom of society; then they will be able to shape those decisions with a view to improving life and making opportunities for people at the bottom. It is only when those responsible can get out of the restrictions of middle-class thinking that change in our society can begin to be phased in.

What Does "Middle Class" Mean?

I think economically the middle class is no longer a homogeneous group. There are some middle class people who are doing very well, while there are others who are struggling. But I certainly wouldn't see the struggle of the poor as being them versus the middle class; that is much too simplistic. It seems to me that there are some working-class families who have far more disposable cash at the end of the week than some middle-class families. There are some working-class families who would be more secure than some middle-class families. I think that what I would really like to see is many middle-class people realising that the way that our society is structured, and the way it is going, is just as much an oppression of them as it is for working-class people. Hopefully then they would see that it is in their interests to change the way society is structured every bit as much as it is in the interests of the poor to change the way society is structured. There is nothing in substantial social change for those who are comfortably off. However, I don't equate the 'haves' with the middle class anymore, because I think there are many amongst the middle class who are in an intermediate category, who are struggling, and they are not in the 'haves' categories. The 'haves' have nothing to gain from a change of structure in society. But a society that believes that everybody should have what is necessary to live a decent human life is in the interests of both the poor and of those middle-class people who are struggling. They could be in the gutter wondering how they are going to feed their kids, wondering where they are going to live, wondering will they ever get a job again.

Oppressors and Oppressed?

I don't see life in terms of oppressor and oppressed, not in an Irish context anyway. Perhaps it is, but I don't see it in those terms within Irish society. I would take the view that every social group is both an oppressor and an oppressed group. The poor oppress one another just as much as middle-class people oppress one another, if you want to talk in those terms. Take people living in Ballymun: while they are oppressed by the structures of society, they are also oppressed because X who lives down the road is breaking into all their houses, or because they can't leave their bicycle outside or it would be gone. And so forth.

My vision of society is one where the number-one priority is that everybody's fundamental rights are guaranteed. By that I mean that everybody has enough food, everybody has adequate housing, everybody has good basic education, good access to health care and that everybody has a job. For the Roman Catholic Church those would be the five fundamental rights. Whatever has to be changed to provide those rights, must be changed, and the aim of the government, and the aim of the majority of people in society, is to ensure that every single human being in that society has those rights given to them. So if we suddenly find a homeless person, or a person without food, it naturally becomes a matter of urgent priority that that particular situation is remedied. The gains for the haves would be on two levels. On a material level, they would live more secure lives, there would be less crime, there would be less violence. I would see this one as the most important. Many of the social problems we have to-day stem from deep feelings of lack of self-respect, deep feelings of being nobody, of being nothing; and that is passed on to people by society. It is given to them in the way they are treated by society and it leads to the sorts of social problems commonly associated with the poor such as crime, violence, sexual abuse, wife-battering, broken homes and that sort of thing. But in a society which guarantees to every human being those fundamental rights, you are in effect giving to each person dignity and self-respect. You are not treating people as second class, and you are not saying to anyone: you are less important than we are. The second concerns the people who are well off and well placed in a society which has so many people who are struggling in poverty.

Dehumanising Effects of Poverty

The well-off don't have a concept of the dehumanising effects of poverty because they are cut off from this experience or aspect of life. It exists in front of them but they don't want to know about it. They can't afford to know about it because if they really knew, and really took it on board and really responded as human beings, they would naturally want to do something. And that would effect their lifestyle. They would have to make sacrifices, they would have to give up things in order to ensure that the situation was remedied. The natural reaction is to insulate oneself, to wear a mask so that you don't see it, so that you don't appreciate it, so that you don't understand it; and that seems to me to be living a lie. By doing that you are telling yourself things that are not true, and you are failing to allow your real human feelings to emerge, to act upon your real deep feelings of compassion, concern and love.

My vision of society is of a society where everyone's fundamental rights are guaranteed. It is not a society where these rights are the consequence of other things, such as people having work or whatever. We must make a commitment to ensure that every human being has these rights, and that whatever other sacrifices we have to make as a society, we will make them to ensure that this happens. I would see the distinction between socialism and capitalism as important. Socialism, for all its faults, sees the providing of these fundamental rights as a direct demand to be made on the government. Capitalism sees it as a consequence of certain other things, particularly a developed economy. Develop the economy properly and sufficiently and everybody will be employed, and as a result of employment all of these other things will fall into place. For me personally, a leaning towards socialism would be more preferable than a leaning towards capitalism. I think no change will come about without the support of many people in the middle class; but on the other hand, change will not come about from the middle class alone. So it would seem to me that change will come about, be it through an alliance between people who are poor and wanting change, and some people in the middle class who are committed to helping them to bring about change. Indeed, they may see it as being in their own interests to bring about change and I certainly believe that the poor must be the fundamental agents in bringing it about.

Escaping from a Prison

In a situation where the poor and the middle class exist side by side, the only way in which middle-class people can cope with that is to deny the existence of the struggling, the homeless, those denied access to education and health care, by rationalising it away. Over a period of time that dehumanises them; because they are blinding themselves, and they lose touch with the reality that actually exists on their doorstep. They live in a world of make-believe they have created for themselves, that excludes these sort of problems. They have to do that because if they face up to the realities, they would have to do something; and ultimately, that something would lead to a radical change in their lifestyle and in the society they are living in. The only alternative to reacting spontaneously and with compassion is to deny that the problem exists and to insulate yourself. And by doing that, I think that you lock yourself up in a prison of your own making. It's a prison that you could walk out of if you wanted to, but choose not to because you are afraid of what you may find outside. You are afraid of what walking outside the gate of that prison might do to the world you have constructed for yourself.

I think middle-class people have a lot of self-confidence. Some times too much. They usually have a sense of being important, a sense of self-respect, a sense of their own dignity. They are often well-educated and have a broad understanding and a broad perspective, and can examine and analyse problems rationally. That might not be found in poorer areas where people may be more spontaneous, angry and less analytical. There is also a gentleness about middle-class people. We are uncomfortable with anger and confrontation and generally try to avoid it, so it can often be congenial being a middle-class member. On the other hand I find there is an artificiality about it and I feel very uncomfortable about it. I do get a sense that I am in prison, that I want to get out and get back to where life is really at.

FINBARR FLOOD

Nobody Calls me Mister

Finbarr Flood was born in Dublin in 1938 and attended the Christian Brothers School in Brunswick Street. He left school at fourteen and joined the Guinness Brewery as a messenger in 1953, working his way through the organisation to become Managing Director of Guinness, Dublin in 1989. He was a professional footballer with Shelbourne, winning a FAI Cup Medal in 1960, and later with Morton F.C. in Scotland and then Sligo Rovers. He is now Chairman of Shelbourne F.C. He is a member of the Institute of Personnel Management, a member of the Labour Relations Commission and a former Vice-President of F.I.E.

My father worked in the brewery. He came in as a messenger as I did. Most of my life was lived around the Oxmanstown Road area known as Kelltown. We lived in Rosse Street, which was a street of cottages, and then moved onto Oxmanstown Road which had an upstairs, and then moved to Manor Street, a three-bedroom house. My whole childhood was lived in an environment of artisan dwellings. People graduated through the establishment, according to the number of children they had. You lived in the cottages with two children, a boy and a girl (or two of the same sex). Once you had got three there was a complication, so you had an opportunity to "trade houses" (or swap houses,) and that was the accepted system in the artisan scene. So when my second sister was born, we had an opportunity to swap with people who had a grown-up family, they moved down to the cottages and we moved up to the upstairs house. I mean that was the environment really. My childhood background would have been influenced by the comfort of the brewery background, which would have been perceived in Dublin as being fairly well provided for. It would have been seen as "womb-to-tomb" protection. Because my father worked in the brewery, we were never in danger of starving, and equally I would say that my father worked hard to provide us with the comforts that we had. When I started working first I earned two pounds ten, which would be fifty shillings. I gave up two pounds, I got ten shillings back in pocket money and half-a-crown of that was put in the Post Office for me so I had seven-and-six. From very early on I was trained to be thrifty, and in fact that probably still comes through in my life, although in my latter years now I might run amuck a bit. I go through a phase where I am conscious of every penny, even when I don't need to be. That's from my background. But I mean we would have had a fairly good diet, week in week out. Thursday was pay day, so Friday was always better than other days; but then, as the week went on, it wasn't that there was any poverty but you saw the difference. Thursday and Friday great. The weekend then. And you were struggling again. People were paid every week, so that is the kind of environment I lived in.

Life of Oxmanstown Road

We lived in a very close-knit community, and looking back on it, we shared a lot of things. It wasn't that people lived in each other's houses but they were always available to help each other. I think the one thing I find about Oxmanstown Road or that kind of environment was a feeling of sharing of success when someone was successful, and a feeling of shared pain if someone was suffering. There wasn't the same ruthless rivalry. If someone did well, you didn't put them down, or try to put them down. There was quite a sharing of success, and I find that still spills over. I still get notes or letters from people who lived or grew up around Oxmanstown Road. I sent in my driving licence recently — into the driving tax office — and I get a note back from a guy I don't even remember: "It is great to see one of the locals doing well". There is nothing on the tax form to indicate my job; he only saw the name, but he remembered. Having an unusual name makes it easier. But it shows the kind of feeling. I meet people around Oxmanstown Road and they are quite pleased I have the job I have. For a Dublin person to be managing the brewery is seen as an achievement for the locality. A lot of people worked around this area, others in the Liberties or across the Liffey, they worked in the brewery and they worked when it was very hard, when times were difficult and when the brewery was very class-ridden.

We shared very similar things. I can still remember sitting on the doorsteps of the cottages listening to Dick Barton, Special Agent, on a Saturday. We sat in the porch, maybe seven to ten of us, listening to the radio inside in someone's house. We would sit there for an hour-and-a-half on a Saturday listening to the omnibus edition of this thing during the week. And that was happiness.

When Rosse Street was Enormous

When we lived in the cottages there was a family called Avers who had a car, that was unheard of in those days, that anyone would have a car in our area. The car was outside the door but if it rained we would all bundle into the car and sit in the car, we were allowed to do that, but you would sit quietly listening to the rain. I still have a feeling of comfort when I hear the rain belting on the window because I grew up in that kind of a cocoon, inside the car. When I say this to people they don't seem to understand what it meant, you know to actually get into a car and sit in it and be allowed to sit there. We sat there silently for maybe an hour, no problem. The whole gang of us who would be seen as not exactly the quietest around the place. We played cricket in the street. There is a wicket in Rosse Street still, on the wall made out of tar that I put there when I was a kid, and I brought my own children up to see it, to see the area, and I have shown them the wicket that is there. We played cricket across the footpath, we played football on the street, we played all sorts of games. To me Rosse Street was a huge street, the cottages were huge, the area was enormous but now you feel you could actually step across, you feel as if you could get up the street in two bounds. The whole thing, the proportions have changed dramatically. It is all different, but when we lived there it was enormous. We didn't go out of Rosse Street to the North Circular Road to play; you weren't allowed to go to the North Circular Road. The North Circular Road was not only dangerous from a traffic point of view, but there was a different type of — what would you call it? — a different bracket of people that lived on the North Circular Road. So you were kept back. You kept away from there.

We had very simple tastes. When I was growing up if you were interested in sport and you got involved in football and things like that, it dominated your life. Everything was about sport, there was no television, there was nothing else, so if you were good at sport you played table tennis, you played soccer or you played ball games on the street and that dominated your whole life.

Teenage Uncertainty

You never felt deprived of anything. Now if you said to me: did you feel very well off? I probably didn't. I mean I was quite happy with what I had. Life was enjoyable. Probably the biggest problem was the uncertainty or insecurity of teenage years. I'm not sure whether people in different surroundings would be much more confident than we were. They probably would be, but then we had the Christian Brothers. I went to the Christian Brothers, and although they were good teachers, I'm not sure if they did anything to instill confidence in the people. I am not running them down; they probably did a good job for me. However, they really didn't balance the educational bit with the whole person bit. A lot of people came out insecure, uncertain, and probably went through their teenage years feeling pretty miserable, without the confidence to mix.

Professional Footballer

I was never really sure about what was success. I would have been very conscious of failure; that would have been quite obvious. But as for success, I never really was conscious of what my parents saw as success for me. In some ways it was a help, because I grew up mad on sport and then became a professional footballer, and I suppose one of the things that helped me was that I was never under any pressure from my family. My father and mother knew nothing about football, so I never knew whether they were proud. I probably sensed that they were proud, but they never really said it to me. It is probably something that your parents don't say to you; you're conscious of it, and they probably would have said it to others; but I was never conscious that they saw my success as a professional footballer, either here or in Scotland, as something that was a major achievement. It is only subsequent years, when I finished playing football, that I would have been aware of the sense of pride they took in it.

Starting at the Brewery

In relation to my career they didn't want me to go into the brewery. They fought like mad to stop me. I left school at fourteen and went in, but they did everything in their power to make sure that didn't happen. They got a number of people up to talk to me who were living in the area and convince me that the right thing to do was to stay on at school.

One of them was Sean Comean who is now the secretary of the Department of Finance. I had lunch with him some months ago and we were just reminiscing about him persuading me that I shouldn't go into the brewery. There was no future for me in the brewery, they said. And in many ways that seemed right, because people came into the brewery at fourteen and at twenty-one all that was facing them was labouring work. There were no opportunities for them.

The brewery was run very much on class lines. The different classes of people, or staff, just didn't mix, and you very seldom passed boundaries. Nobody could have imagined that, in the years ahead, it would all change and a person like myself would get the opportunity to come through and be Managing Director of the brewery. That would have been unheard-of in those days.

I am not sure exactly what they would have seen as a success. I think that they would probably see my present position as success alright, particularly my father and both my grandfathers who worked here. My family would be quite proud of what I have achieved and what has happened to me. But I wouldn't have been conscious of what was success. I was never under pressure. Nobody ever said to me that I must do x, y and z.

There were no goodies given out, but there was certainly punishment given out. My father used his tie. My father wasn't adverse to taking his tie off and using it whenever he needed to. But I don't remember any goodies being dished out as a reward. We were always conscious that if you were in trouble, you could go home. And I think that is a very important factor. If I was in trouble, I would head home. I mean I would have always been conscious that, no matter what I did, although the initial outburst might be bad, I could always go back. And even in later years I would always go back. I never had a feeling that I could not go home — no matter what I would do, or what crime I would commit. Now I might get hell kicked out of me, but then I would be protected. I wouldn't have had a fear that I couldn't have gone home, although my father was very strict and a difficult person to understand. My mother would have been different, and after the initial fear of the problem, I would have felt that everything would be okay.

What Makes Me Tick?

I am not conscious of ever having to bottle up my feelings. I am equally not conscious of ever letting them go.

I often wonder what dictated my own make-up. What actually made me the way I am? I think I am quite difficult to operate with, I am a bit unreasonable, I am unreasonable in my demands of people and what I want. I don't always make it clear to people that they are people whom I respect deeply. I drive people hard. I don't drive people hard that don't have sufficient in them to be driven, but I would probably be very hard on people that I have great confidence in. But it is quite confusing for them at times, because they see it as if I am hammering hell out of them but my inner thing is that I don't have any doubts about them at all. I think that is one big failing in myself. I assume that people know what I think of them, when in fact that is not always true. I probably don't tell people how highly I regard them, in fact I would probably go the opposite way. I am probably much harder on people that I think very highly of, because I am driving them, not to get more but because I believe that we can achieve something together. It does cause great problems to people because they don't understand why they are getting hammered and somebody else, who maybe contributes far less either to my personal life or even to my work life, seems to be having an easier time.

In a way maybe that goes back to childhood. Things were done in a particular way in the environment where I lived in around Oxmanstown Road. Families were cocooned a bit, but it might not have necessarily been put up in lights: "we love you".

Football Wanes, Guinness Waxes

When I came into the brewery first, given how class-ridden the place was, you have no idea what that did to your confidence. Your confidence was at a very low ebb. You were called by your surname; you had no rights; you were inspected every morning in your uniform, to make sure that everything was in order, that your buttons and all were shining. I was put on "Charge 7" twice (at least) for looking contemptuously at my superior. I remember spending one Saturday morning in the director's boardroom with Sir Charles Harvey, who was a great man. He was one of the first to start to break the barriers in here, and my task for the whole morning was to turn the pages of a manual. He read the manual like that and nodded, and I turned the page. Now that was the kind of subservient role you played in the brewery and that had a dreadful effect on your confidence. You had to have some outlet from that kind of environment and for some it came in rebelling against it, others left the brewery, others went outside with their talents to use elsewhere. I overcame it because I was doing very well at football, so therefore the brewery and what was happening in the brewery was of no great consequence to me. It was a way of eating properly; you were getting a salad there, but really football was my life in those days. It was only as my football career started to wane that my Guinness career started taking off. I was very lucky really; when one finished the other started to take off. But you would have had to have worked in the brewery those days to understand what it could do to your confidence.

Don't Buck the System

Our parents grew up — whether they were aware of it or not — with a kind of subservient approach to things. You didn't question your superiors, you didn't buck the system, you didn't stand up and be counted. I remember in first babies, in the convent up here, trying to do it in an art class with a teacher, cutting these "gainsays" out of newspapers, and I couldn't cut it. I remember roaring crying. The teacher kept back ten of us in the class after hours. I was being made conform with the way things were done. Now you get the total reverse to what we did there. We conformed, and we were brought up to conform, and if you broke out of that it was seen as unacceptable. I think that was the biggest weakness of living in that environment. I see people now who are very rebellious and they come through, standing up on their own, and they put their own stamp on things. I have a great admiration for them. Not the ones that go off and wreck things, but people who actually come out of a system where their personality has come through and they have actually survived somebody trying to put them into a mould, put them into a pattern. I think the single weakness was that we grew up in an environment where the rules were laid down. You followed the rules, you didn't break the rules, you didn't query them, you didn't balk at them and you conformed. That was probably the biggest negative, in that it stifled initiative in people and probably sapped their confidence. They didn't realise there was another world, and that you could do things and you could get outside. Yet having said that, the number of people I meet, who have come out of that environment and have done very well, is quite surprising. So within that environment there were enough people of independent mind to actually come through and show they were as good as others. You were led to believe that this was your place and no further should you go, and a number of people just pushed out the barriers. They either rebelled or got there in a quieter way, but they got there. On the other hand, I often wonder how many of the people who lived in that area and grew up in the type of environment in Dublin that I did, how many of them could have done an awful lot better if they had been given the confidence to match their ability. The ability was there, but the confidence was lacking, and you needed both. You obviously needed good luck as well.

Table Tennis with Protestants

I don't have early memories on social class to any great extent, because up to the time I came to work in the brewery at fourteen I lived and moved within the same kind of environment, the same kind of people whether I was going to school or whether it was around the area I lived in. The one thing that I was conscious of was Protestants. In our area there were two Protestant families, the Gambles and the Evans. Both families were highly respected, but the kind of belief that prevailed in those days was that Protestants were all doomed and would never go to Heaven. You couldn't visit a Protestant church, and all the rest. It fascinated me subsequently to look back and think how those families, living in a totally Catholic environment, established themselves as well as they did in the area. There were probably other Protestants, but they were the only two I was conscious of, because they were people with whom I used to play. They always seemed to have a little more than the rest of us, although they lived in the cottages. They had a plot joining the house and they had a table-tennis table. At night time you might be invited up to play table tennis, which was a treat because there were sweets, cakes, and the tennis. So you were conscious that they seemed to have a little more, and they also seemed to have what I perceived to be quite a Christian outlook. They never seemed to be involved in any problems or any difficulties, and they were the only ones that I would have been conscious of as people who were different.

Houses with Steps

I was probably conscious too, that if you moved onto the North Circular Road, people were more superior. What superior meant, I would not have a clue. Other than they had steps up to their houses, and the houses were quiet, and nobody ever seemed to come out of them. They seemed to be sinister or menacing, but I wouldn't have had a clue what superior meant. I was conscious they were superior alright but it could have meant any number of things. I would have been definitely conscious of it, but in terms of meeting and mixing with people I would have been with the same type of people right through childhood and school. Playing football was a great leveller. You didn't know who the hell you were playing against, you hadn't a clue whether the person you were playing against was middle-class, upper-class, poor or whatever. Most people were either the poor or the middle-class, but class didn't enter into it. You knew you would die for the same people on the team, you didn't know whether they were black, white, Protestant, no one knew, you knew it was just whether they could play football or you could beat them, and that probably broke down a lot of class barriers.

Everyone in a Box

Class-wise the brewery was a totally different world. I mean everybody was in their own little box. People were classified under different headings. The monthly paid staff were known as staff, and they were an extremely elitist group. The senior managers in those days, usually came in at about ten o'clock in the morning and went home at four in the afternoon. They sat and read their *Irish Times* and in some cases they had their slippers, but they didn't deal with problems or anything else. I am sorry about that because, when my turn came, the whole thing had reversed, and I am in first now and probably last out as well. That is one of the things that has changed in the brewery. I think everybody accepts that the senior managers work long and hard, whereas in the past they didn't. Even within the staff there were five categories of staff. There was number one staff, two staff, gate staff, laboratory staff and unclassified staff. And none of them mixed. They were very class-conscious. Then you had the weekly paid, who were different to everyone else. There was no question of any movement between them, and you became very conscious of your place and whether you were doing an "upstairs" or a "downstairs". When you think of me sitting in the boardroom turning the pages for the director all Saturday morning and not a word, just a nod, I mean it was "upstairs, downstairs".

Over there, or across the road in ninety-eight which was the house just beyond the power station, lived the M.D. of the brewery. They used to have dances on the lawn in the summer for the staff with males and females dancing on the lawn from four o'clock to six o'clock and then they would adjourn. That was how it was. There was no way any of us would have been in any way invited. I opened the doors and took the coats. That was my role over there, for which I was rewarded with ten shillings which was very generous in those days. It was very class-conscious and you really had to have a rebellious streak in you to kind of live and survive.

Harbouring Resentment

I would have expected most of the young people whom I grew up with in here to have resentment in them. It wouldn't have been visible; they might not have been conscious of it. It wouldn't be something that ate into you, but it certainly was there. You know that resentful attitude, but then you were resentful coming out of the Christian Brothers too. About most things, anyway. I think there was a fair resentment, but a subdued resentment. People didn't show it, I mean they conformed. Inwardly you might be seething at times, but you didn't let it show.

I am not sure you would have perceived anything positive of the top bods, except that, as in any environment, some were very nice people who would be helpful. And the company itself was very positive. The brewery would pay for people to go on and educate themselves, and that was part of the attraction of coming in here; that you could do your study at night.

Our parents probably grew up to conform. Now my father could be quite narky in his own way, and probably a lot of my narkiness and my short fuse came from my father who would not let anybody drive him. He would accept the rules, or whatever, but he would never let anyone walk on him, and was quite a terrier in rebelling. I suppose only in later years did I begin to realise that some of that was in me. It wouldn't have been a conscious decision that it was a class thing against which he was going to rebel. It was a bit of arrogance or a belief that he was good at what he did. He was well able to stand up and be counted.

I don't remember my parents looking enviously at anybody or being down-hearted because somebody else had such and such.

48

When my parents got married they had very little. They didn't have a house, they were in a flat, they didn't have furniture, they started from very little. As they got established in later years and they had a house and they had their own furniture, even if the house was rented, they were probably very contented with what they had, and rightly so, but there was no envy. I didn't grow up with a feeling of envy, I grew up with a feeling of believing, but probably initially not believing that I could be good or I could do things, but just getting on with what I had to do. Things seemed to evolve.

School was a Disaster

The subject of "haves and have nots" certainly wasn't touched on. No, I would say school was a disaster in terms of personal development. Academically it was very good. One of the reasons I had a problem leaving school was that at that stage there was a primary certificate. Now the primary certificate had English, Irish and arithmetic in it; there were three subjects only and there were two hundred marks for each and I went to Brunswick Street. I went to Brunor. I had Paddy Crosby for five years and when the results of the primary came out, I had got full marks in the primary in everything, unheard of and never to be got again as he said. I can never understand how I got them because part of that was a composition in English and in Irish, so how you could get a hundred percent in a composition? I could never understand it but it came out that way, and that made it even more difficult for me to get out of school. They were determined that I shouldn't leave, that I should go on to university and everything else. But all of the schooling I remember was the academic side. There was nothing about the development of the person. Most of the fellows I grew up with hadn't a clue what life was about. They really didn't. They weren't prepared at all.

I would always have been conscious that there are always people worse off, in fact that would have been one of the things which was drilled into me at home; the poor people and how badly off they were. Looking back on it — there was very little looking upwards! — it was all pointing out how well off we were, because of the others who were less fortunate.

I wouldn't have been in contact with poor people, but I would have seen them around the area. I can remember people with no shoes as I grew up. My grandmother lived in Thomas Street. I used to come from Oxmanstown Road over to Thomas Street as a child across the Liffey. I would have been very conscious of the people around the Liberties, and there was quite a degree of poverty. A poor person to me would have been someone with ragged clothes, no shoes and just not well looked after.

At home you wouldn't hear anything derogatory about the poor. All you would hear were things of pity, concern and, you know, a sadness really. It was never said that they could do better, or should do better. It was sympathy, and how lucky we were.

Still Only One Initial

I don't perceive that, since childhood, I have moved social class at all. I mean I don't have a mental feeling that I have moved from one class to another. I feel that I am still in the same group. I still mix with the same type of people, I still have only one initial. I really don't genuinely feel any difference in class or otherwise. I am still only conscious of the less well-off. This is not to say that I do anything about it. But I would be more conscious of those who have nothing, or are not as lucky as I am, than the people that I perceive as having the things I want. I don't really have any great designs or awareness of those who have more than I have, so it hasn't really changed me. Anything you gain is only on loan, and you are only as good as your last success, and that will be short-lived.

I would be quite surprised if people who grew up with me would see me as having moved up a social class bracket. They might see me as being financially better off, but I don't believe anybody would perceive me as being in a different bracket. I see myself as being more comfortable and having more money, less money worries than I might have had early on, but I don't see myself as being any different to anybody else who gets married, takes on a mortgage, struggles for a few of years, then your children are grown up and things begin to get easier. From that point of view financially I probably am in a better bracket than I was but not in social class. Nobody calls me mister. I have never met anybody who calls me mister, inside the brewery or outside. I have never been called mister.

My Dublin accent hasn't even changed. I did the Pat Kenny show one night and talked about coming from the bottom up, and I got numerous letters, saying to hear somebody with a Dub accent running the brewery was unbelievable. People think that, if you have a Dublin accent, you should be in the lower class.

Work in the Department

I was lucky enough to work in a department. The manager of the day, a guy called Harry Hannon, actually tried to break down the barriers that existed by giving people from what was known as the shop floor an opportunity to go on the staff. He opened up four positions in his department for people to apply for. I initially didn't get one of those four positions. I was in the last eight. I was the favourite to get one of those positions but failed to get it, and I can tell you that was one of the biggest disappointments of my life. Subsequently, one of the people dropped out. And I got the job and that was the first break that I got on the staff. After that I was lucky to work with people in a department where part of the process was to give people their heads. It was led by a guy who had the ability to motivate people. Then in 1977 I was brought into the personnel department by Paddy Galvin and Brian Walsh, and they saw things were changing in the brewery and there was a need to bring in a new style of management. When I went to personnel I hated the place, but afterwards I settled down and things just seemed to take off. I couldn't say there was any single thing. I just became personnel manager, and then personnel director, and then Managing Director.

The members of the staff had their own class distinctions. In 1967, when I arrived, there were still great barriers. People had their own fixed tables in the dining room where they sat year in and year out. You didn't just go in and sit down. You had to wait to be seated, so it was quite a strain initially. But once there was a strike in 1974 in this company, and after that things were never the same. The barriers came down very rapidly after that. People realised they needed to depend on each other, that they lived in a community that was too small to have all these barriers. So over the next twenty years it changed dramatically. Now it is a different place altogether.

Class Distinctions

Separate dining rooms was one way class distinction worked. There was also insecurity. You had lived in a very subservient way for years, and it's difficult to change that. Some of the people here, because of that background, were never really able to shake off the feeling of inferiority. I think if you were lucky enough to get through, to get a few jumps reasonably quickly, you began to get your confidence. If you didn't have that, you really had a problem. But I don't believe any of that operates now. I would defy anyone to actually say that I make class distinctions in the brewery. People might say I have a car out in the yard, and that that is a class distinction. I would see that as part of the package. But in terms of class distinctions or the aristocratic tendencies, none of that is there.

I never had any problems or strains with family or childhood friends for moving up the ranks. I never had the slightest difficulty like that, and if I had I was never aware of it. Certainly I don't think it has come from my side at all. I take a great pride in the fact that I have the job I have, and I passionately believe in the company that I run and the people who work here.

The Boss is a Loner

When you become boss, you become a loner. I have no problems socialising and all the rest, but because of the nature of the job, it is very lonely. You don't have anybody, apart from your secretary, who is the key to your survival. But not only that, the knowledge you have, the inputs and the pressures to deliver makes it very lonely. It is not something you can share. You can share with your colleagues some information, but you can't give everybody all of the information, the problems, the worries, the concerns, and the dependencies of people on you. You know people are depending on you to actually portray the company in a particular way, a positive way.

Particularly in a company like ours, where Guinness Dublin was the home of Guinness and is now part of a multi-national and therefore is a much smaller fish in the pond. You have all those pressures of keeping people happy, motivated and feeling that the Guinness they grew up with is still there.

But here in the brewery it is not a question of projecting a good image, it is a pressure to project a professionalism in what we do. "Guinness Dublin is the best" and I mean to keep that pressure on people, and to keep people believing in that puts its own pressure on you. People might find it very difficult to understand the loneliness of being a managing director of a company. I think it must be the same whether the company is big or small.

You can't afford to let people see the pressures you are under, because the one thing they don't want to see is uncertainty. They don't want to know what it is like for the captain of the industry. I have often thought if people saw who was on the bridge, or how the bridge was being operated, they would get off the ship. People want to know that the boss is human. They do, up to a point, but they don't want to see that the individual managing the company (or the team managing the company) is uncertain. You have got to make sure that you project an image of professionalism, something that they can take pride in. And that is an enormous pressure.

Not that I feel pressure in the job. Not at all. I don't have any worries about the job. I can do the job with my eyes closed. It is not a problem. It is more, I suppose, the social pressure of the responsibility that you have for so many people to just make sure they feel that they are part of something that is worthwhile. That is what puts pressure on you, more than the commercial aspect. On the commercial side you plan, you organise, you hit rocky water and you get off and go back again. The other bit is what you miss, the ability to sit down with a group of people and say: I am in terrible trouble on this. You don't have that, you know.

The Right Place at the Right Time

There are people who would be equally talented as I am (or am perceived to be), who have not got the breaks, so therefore have not moved. Even in the brewery there were lots of very talented people who just didn't get the breaks. A lot of success in life is being in the right place at the right time and selling a particular product that people want to buy. I could come back in ten or fifteen years and the talents and the strengths that I may be perceived to have may not be what this company wants, so I could languish anywhere in the company. I was just lucky that what I was perceived to have was needed by the company at that point in time.

Helping people move up the ladder rates very high on my conscience as well as my agenda, and probably more on my conscience than my agenda. Because, like everyone else, I am full of good intentions. I am conscious of how lucky I am, how privileged I have been and how unfortunate others are. And any opportunities I get where people put things in front of me, I try to respond.

As for social class, I don't have a particular sense of belonging in any categorised grouping or any categorised area. I still have a problem with small talk. Whether that comes from my background or not I don't know. Others say that it doesn't come across, that I seem totally relaxed, but I am not. Some people are brilliant, they can hold a conversation on trivia; but I can't do that. I suppose if somebody is telling me about themselves and it is of interest then I can be right with them, but I cannot generate the small talk. It is a talent which I don't possess.

I Have this Classless Feeling

I think class is about confidence really in a way. The one thing that we were taught was that you were to remember your place and there were rules. I think from my understanding of working-class people, they are mentally geared to stay in the box, stay down and accept their position. I don't know if that is a fact or not, but that seems to be it. Surprisingly you get some people with great guts breaking out of it, but they are the exception.

Politics

Politics, in my mind, is about running a company, only that the "company" happens to be Ireland. It is no different from running the brewery. I see people with massive obligations and pressure on them to actually look after all of the community in whatever way they can. The reality of it is that we live in a greedy society. We are greedy. We pay lip service to everybody having everything. But realistically we look after our own patch. We grew up in a world of sharing. If someone was sick, people were in all day looking after them. But it doesn't seem to operate now. It operates with young people much stronger than it did in my generation, or even I would say in my parents' generation. The younger people are much more conscious and prepared to help the underprivileged than we were, I don't think we were very good at that.

Guinness And The Colonial Style

Guinness was organized more or less on the colonial style — the generals, the officers and the non-commissioned officers, etc. That seems to be the way it operated. There were different divisions, different classes of people, different levels. And it wasn't just based on job responsibility. It was based on a very privileged — no, privileged is probably not the word to use — it was based on a historical class base.

The changes started coming in the seventies, when Guinness in Ireland began to be aware that it had a problem with the competition from different beers (coming into Ireland), different products. The fact was that the Guinness group, over the years probably had not put the investment into Dublin that was required, and the plant was now beginning to need replacement. The whole world was changing. In the old days the product seemed to sell itself and the money poured in. It was now a much more commercial and competitive world and things had to change, and the development plan came in. In the early seventies, a compulsory retirement age of fifty-five came out of the blue and it was quite a traumatic period, because people expected to be here until they were sixty-five, and then suddenly they were told they were gone at fifty-five. There was no choice; it wasn't voluntary; you were just gone. I remember some of the best drivers leaving. They were just shattered, and it was quite a difficult period of time. Out of that came the whole requirement for a different type of management, a much more commercially-aware business sense was required. The company just had to change.

Class stratification didn't make business sense, because you had people in boxes and therefore people couldn't contribute across various disciplines and boxes. They were kept isolated. We had a strike in 1974, the first in two hundred years, and the problem was no one knew how to fix it. There was a lack of intercommunication between groups and categories. Now, if we get into trouble, people will get together. We have a brewery council where all the categories sit together, so there is a forum for people to mix. The brewery council was probably one of the single most effective ways of breaking down the barriers, because once people started to mix in this council and sitting on sub-councils, they were socialising and mixing.

In terms of class, you would probably find that there are some people in the brewery who still have advantages. The regular staff have advantages over those paid on a weekly basis. The only difference of any significance is the hours they work. The staff works thirty-seven-and-a half and the weekly-paid work thirty-nine. The rest of the benefits are almost the same, but there is a perception that it is bigger than it actually is. Over the years there probably has been more harmonisation of conditions and working arrangements.

Problems with the Unions

The one thing we haven't got is open advertisement and movement between the groups, but strangely enough it is because the unions failed to agree to it. The company would like to open up opportunities to everyone. If there is a job, the best person gets it all the time. That creates a difficulty for the seniority concept within the trade union movement. The craft unions and SIPTU have not accepted it. We would like to open up opportunities. People should be able to go in from the staff to other areas as well, so there is a feeling that everybody wants what everybody else has, but no one is going to give up anything that they have.

We have been able to progress from a very uncompetitive capital-deprived company to one with massive capital investment and high-technology, seen now as probably one of the most efficient production units in the group, and also respected around the world as the leader in innovation and brewing technology. The brewing and innovation on this site is more advanced than anywhere else. We have people coming from Japan and America and everywhere else to look at it. The benefits from the employees point of view is that we have managed to preserve the Guinness package: good pay, high earnings and other benefits like the medical department, free catering, that kind of thing. This package, while there has been some minor changes in it, overall it is seen as a very good package. We don't have a massive turnover of people. Quite the reverse. The other thing is that people now in the company are shareholders, they are paid in shares every year. The Guinness share price transferred from cash profit shares to actual shares nearly five years ago. The share price of Guinness at that stage was about £3, and it is now £9.80. People who got shares then, can now start picking up quite a tidy profit. And that is every year now. So the growth in the Guinness share price has been phenomenal over the last few years and everybody is sharing in that.

JOE DUFFY

Ballyfermot to Donnybrook and Back

Joseph Duffy was born in Ballyfermot. After short stints as a shop assistant and bell boy he become one of the first beneficiaries of free second-level eduction. Two years after finishing his Leaving Cert he began studying Economics and Social Science in TCD, where as president of the Students Union he spent two highly publicised weeks in Mountjoy Prison over the government's refusal to give medical cards to all students. He has since become one of the best known voices of Irish radio, for both his own shows and his work with Gay Byrne.

When you are growing up you never perceive your family other than what they are. You don't know that you are working-class, or lower-working-class or middle-class or whatever. We lived in Ballyfermot, which has been characterised as a large suburban working-class estate, so we were working-class, I suppose. My father had a normal job. He was a packer in Glen Abbey, which was a knitwear factory. He ran the dispatch department. And my mother was bringing up six kids, so she worked even harder at home.

As you are growing up, you think that your standard of living is adequate. You know no different; you know no better; you have only one childhood. Our standard of living was a constant, I think. I was always well fed, and I can never remember being hungry. I remember the big moment was my father's pay day, on Fridays you could buy chocolate. And you had dessert on a Sunday, and you didn't have it on any other day of the week. When I was quite young my father was working in England. But

I can never remember being hungry or going to bed hungry or not having a shoe on my foot. Neither can I remember being embarrassed about my clothing.

Doctor Who? Doctor Who

Next door had a car, and they also had an aerial on the roof, so they could get all the stations on the television which we didn't have and they use to talk about Dr. Who and I would say Who? and they would say Dr. Who, and I would think they were slagging me, but they weren't. We had a telly; it was one of those things you put the ten pence in the slot. It might go just before the end of the programme, but by the time you got the ten pence the programme was over. So you didn't know if the baddie got killed. Actually what I was more jealous of was they also had a dog called Ringo.

I suppose it is the hope of every parent that their children do better than they did. They fight for that. We were not pestered from an early age, and it was not a feature of my growing up or of my psyche that I had to do better. There was absolutely no pressure, no oppressive pressure on that front as far as I was concerned. I wasn't over-conscious of having to do good, bad or indifferent.

Success for me would have been a job. I was very conscious during summers of trying to get a job and it was difficult to get one, especially when you were only four years of age! My brother got a job with the Swastika Laundry, which was a great achievement. He wanted to stay on, not go back to school. A couple of my brothers left school at their Inter Cert and got jobs, and that was regarded as being a good achievement — the job rather than the education. I left when I did my Leaving Certificate and then went to work immediately. I worked for three years, and then I wanted to go to college. My father was worried, not about the cost of going to college, but the absence of my income in the house. Obviously the job was more important than third level education.

The way of winning approval was good behaviour. My mother was very strict in discipline and on our behaviour, particularly in relation to adults. If you got into a fight on the street my mother would not go out and take your side if, say, the other mother had come out. She did not take your side against other adults. She would come out and remonstrate with us for getting into trouble. Likewise, if you ever back-answered an adult, regardless of what the adult had said to you, you would be in trouble. Also helping around the house and doing the windows was a way of getting rewarded. Approval didn't depend on getting good marks, but on doing basic stuff in the house.

There wasn't enormous evidence of people kissing each other every morning as they went to work, or as you went to school. It was not that feelings were encouraged or discouraged. It was just that the example was not there.

As for anger, you could lose the head, but I don't know if tantrums got you very far, because my mother was a very strong woman and would take no nonsense.

There wasn't a lot of shouting and it wasn't incredibly cerebral either. It was more a disciplinarian scenario, rather than sit-down-and-argue-things-out. No one threw himself through the window if things went wrong. It was more a middle course: this is wrong behaviour, and just stop it because it will get you nowhere. My mother would be very persistent. She would remember if you did something wrong. You would be disciplined for it. One day when she was in town on a Saturday, we broke one of the glass doors in a China cabinet. She came home at six o'clock, it was a long time after the event and to us it had died down. Eventually we knew she would find out, and we knew that there would be hell to pay. We couldn't hold it in, we had to tell her the minute she came in. She was only getting off the bus across the road and we ran over to tell her, almost with a view to let's get this over with. She is going to find out and she is going to go berserk and it doesn't matter if it happened ten years ago, once she finds out she will go berserk. So we told her, and she went berserk.

I don't go for this guff that there is some nobility in being working-class, or there is some intrinsic worth in being middle-class. I mean we are what we are because of various forces. I see no advantage in being working-class, nor any disadvantage either.

I'm not aware of a particular strength that exists in a working-class milieu that doesn't exist in a middle-class milieu. Take contacts for example. Contacts are important because you develop a network, and this network is as important and as powerful in a working-class area as it would be in a middle-class area. It is not adequate to say that the networks are better in the middle-class. They are not better. The networks in the middle-class area are middle-class networks, and the networks in the working-class area are working-class networks. That's all.

The School I Never Went To

Ironically for me the biggest influence in my life was the Tech in Ballyfermot, which is the school I didn't go to. I went to St. John's College in Ballyfermot. Because I had done a little bit better academically, my mother thought I could go to the "Secco". My brothers went to the Tech. My next door neighbours went to the Tech. My friends went to the Tech. And while I was doing my Leaving Cert, I did night classes in the Tech. It's a weird experience, to be going to one school and doing grinds in another.

However it was from the people that we (myself, my brothers and my friends) met in the Tech — the teachers there were a young group and very progressive — that I became involved in youth clubs, summer projects and the Catholic Youth Council. And I became interested in going back to third level education. I got to know people who had gone through and said it was the easiest thing in the world, which it turned out to be. So strangely the biggest influence on me in terms of moving on was the school I never went to. And the most oppressive thing on me would be the school I did go to, St. John's College in Ballyfermot. They had a career guidance teacher, I went to him and gave him some guff because I had seen Frank Grimes on the Late Late Show going on about being the star in the new film St. Francis of Assisi. And I told this guy that I wanted to be an actor. He ended up convincing me that I wanted to be a bank clerk in Allied Irish Banks. There was no mention of going on to third level education. There was only one person who went on as far as I know, straight from school. He was a doctor's son from outside the area. It was taken as given that he should be going onto third level education. To us it was almost like saying that he should be going to another country, to Tasmania; and I did not know where the boat started from or whether you flew or what, but he went, and that is what I am saying: the deciding factor about whether to go on or not, did not come from within the house. The home was just one of many influences in my life.

I didn't have much sense of other social classes. All my relations were living in Kilbarrack, Coolock, Crumlin, Inchicore, the lower end of Ballyfermot and Cabra. I had no relations outside of Dublin. In other words no rural relations; I hadn't ever been on a farm. I remember being very thrilled with the whole notion of getting up early, as on a farm, at the break of day. My father was a very early riser and I am an early riser as well. It is something I love, and it is something to do with that aspiration or that feeling that I would love to be on a farm, to get up and go out and do the cows, even though that I have no skills in that area.

Kisses and Piano Lessons

I remember one uncle came back from England and bought a house in Raheny. We went out to his house that night, and the priest came to bless it. They had only just moved in. That would have struck me as being different. Another difference was that we lived right beside shops, the chip shop, the newsagents and Boylans. Boylan ran a shop and lived above it. I had become quite friendly with Peter, his son there. I was conscious of them having a car, a phone and things like that. But he went to the same school as we did, and he played the same games as we did and all that carry on. Only now am I going through what I would call a Dublin 4 childhood. I am learning the piano, because I was always interested in music and have recently bought a keyboard piano. I am trying to learn how to play tennis, because I want to look after my health. I am playing squash. There was one Saturday there when I was going to a piano lesson and I was going to tennis and I was up here in Donnybrook and I said to somebody: this is my idea of what a Dublin 4 childhood would be like. On a Saturday you go to your tennis lesson, and then you go over to your piano lesson, and you would be driven from one to another. It is not till later in life that you begin to see these things.

People who heard me on radio might be surprised that I never had elocution lessons. The reason is that in the primary school we went to, which was in Palmerstown because the De La Salle didn't have any space, you had to pay for the elocution lesson. There was either drill, which was sixpence or elocution which was sixpence too. Some fellows did both but I never went to an elocution lesson, and I don't think we ever went to drill because the sixpence just wasn't there.

We never had contact with middle-class people, believe it or not. I had a notion that they were more emotional than we were, in other words that the children would have been kissed every morning when they went to school, and kissed again before they went to bed. That would be the main thing actually; the material difference was not a powerful thing for me.

I remember one of the guys I met in school, who lives in Chapelizod, down the hill from Ballyfermot but up the social-mobility scale. I stayed with him one night, and on leaving the following morning was quite taken aback that his mother kissed him. I cannot remember much about the house in terms of material things, but the kiss was very different and that to me would have characterised the difference.

Stuck with Parents

The experience made me feel jealous. I presume it is similar for all kids. We all want to have something, we all want to have someone else's parents, we all want a John F. Kennedy and a Jackie Onassis as our parents, rather than the two that we were stuck with. I wanted the teacher to be like somebody on T.V. or Gay Byrne and Kathleen Watkins. That would be a kind of childhood fantasy. I'm conscious of people being annoyed by him at times, or saying: he shouldn't be on the air, that is not the voice of Ireland. But I would never have been conscious of that sort of thing as a child.

I would have been conscious of people being worse off, rather than better off, like travellers. I wouldn't have been overly conscious of people being much better off, apart from the doctor, because he had a car. I am not intimidated by people. There were people starting to go to the stew house, as we called it in Ballyfermot, or to collect turf. There were turf dockets. We did that sometimes as well, I hasten to add. But it wasn't a regular gig. I would have been conscious of it, and that would have always struck a cord with me, of people having to go to the stew house, and the sadness. There is a sadness too about people not having their father around.

At home and at school we would have the usual black baby vibes, and I was aware of the St. Vincent De Paul but they never came to our house as it happened. We had a youth club right opposite us which we joined. It was run by the St. Vincent De Paul, and subsequently we got involved in the Conference of St. Vincent De Paul. Every Saturday we used to go to visit old people down in the home in Cork Street, and that would be kind of your social awakening in terms of being conscious that some people did not have family, did not have tobacco or whatever they needed.

If my life was to be put on graph paper, obviously in class terms it would point upwards. But that is the same for the vast majority, thankfully. We are all better off than we were when we were younger. I am better off than my mother was when she was the same age as me, in that we have a TV, a car and all that stuff. Ninety-nine people out of a hundred would say the same.

Why Up?

The essential move, was the decision to go back to third level to continue my education. That decision I can trace clearly back to the arrival of the Tech in Ballyfermot. That process, which began by me coming into contact with that particular building and the people in it, is the single most important thing which has happened me. And I would say the single most important thing which happened to a lot of people where I came from. That is where I wanted to go, and that is very linear and very concrete. It is not a mystery to me how I made that change.

I was the first ever in my family to go to third level. There was no history of it whatsoever. I was the first actually to go beyond Inter even by getting to my Leaving Cert., I was taking a significant jump above and beyond my relations and my fore-fathers. And then to go on to third level was an enormous jump. Thankfully other people have done it since. Even within my own extended family. It was due to the Tech, the teachers in the Tech, getting involved in Ballymun, moving down and running a summer project in Ballymun, getting interested in social work, discovering university and going to university to do social work. They were the jumps.

Will I? or Won't I?

People were mainly encouraging, I mean the discouragements came from within my own head.

I was going out with a woman in Ballymun at the time, and I was trying to make up my mind whether to go to college. It meant giving up the job and money.

I sat on the 36A, which began in Sandyhill Gardens. It was a single decker bus. I said to myself: I will judge this by the number of traffic lights that are either green or red. If the number of traffic lights that are red exceeds the number of traffic lights that are green that means no that I should not go to college; and if the number of traffic lights that are green exceeds the number of red that means yes. I can tell you quite honestly that by the time I got to Parnell Square the number that were red greatly exceeded the number that were green, but I still went to college and just ignored it. But I was into that type of thought process: will I? won't I? I will, I won't.

Family factors that helped the process were the acquiescence of my mother, which blanked out the gentle discouragement of my father. She said let him! let him! He wants it. There is no hassle. My father would have said: where is the money going to come from? I had saved. I had worked for three years. But the absence of the income, that was the problem.

I knew that no grants would be available because I didn't have four honours. I had five honours, but I got three in the second one and I previously got two in the Tech, and you needed four honours in one sitting. In other words a working-class person has to be more intelligent than the middle class. I know quite clearly in my head that the two honours I got in the Tech subsequently were a breeze, absolutely a breeze. I got an A in Business Organisation and an A in Economics, studying them at night. They were no bother to me, and if John's in Ballyfermot had spoken to us about the option of third level, I could have easily got four honours then, and got a grant.

Trinity Opens a Gate

I was not conscious of someone's class. The people in Trinity would have been classified as being well-off. Classification was not based on them, it was based on their parents, and that is a critical difference to make. When I went in I wasn't conscious of saying: this guy is middle-class. There were one or two people you heard of whose father was in a Bank or owned whatever company, but it wasn't an over-riding force of Trinity. But there weren't many people from Ballyfermot in the place but as far as I was concerned that did not disenfranchise the other people in the college or delegitimatise their position in the college.

I had gone to college after a number of years working. At school I had not been academically brilliant by any stretch of the imagination, and I reckoned it was going to be difficult.

I spent the first year in the library studying, and made no new friends. Looking back on it now, that whole thing of going to college and going through the process of getting into Trinity was a very lonely experience. There was no one ringing up on my behalf. I was calling up and down to the registrars office with enquiries. I decided to go into the job and say that I was handing in my notice, and explained that I wanted to go to college. The main strain on me was study, even though I was quite good at it. I became very disciplined studying, at marking out my week and studying quite hard on a regular basis from early morning to late at night. Saturdays and even some Sundays.

No, the strains that emerged were between me and the group of people who subsequently became the major force of the college. Ironically it was the college authorities' perception of us as being working-class that was much more beast-like than our perceptions of them as being middle-class, and they were totally exaggerated in the view of what they thought we were. We were not what they thought we were. The way they reacted was totally over the top, and in turn generated an atmosphere that the college was trying to smash this group of people. It was characterised in the media as if they were just getting rid of working-class people.

The thing that got me involved (when I did get involved) was the statement by the board of Trinity that, with the opening of the new gate to Trinity in Nassau Street, when the arts block was built, that this meant that Trinity was finally open to the people of Dublin. I was acutely conscious that there were two other people along with me from Ballyfermot among the six- thousand student population of Trinity and the forty-five thousand population of Ballyfermot. I wrote a letter, and somebody else wrote back giving out about the chip on my shoulder; then somebody else wrote back, and it just got a lot of us talking in there. It came from first year sociology and social work.

The Ballyfermot — Trinity Nexus

I didn't feel any strain with middle-class students. There was only three from Ballyfermot in it, and that was three guaranteed votes, but we were elected in one of the biggest voting turnouts up to then. So obviously I didn't feel alienated from them, and they didn't feel alienated from me.

I had decided to leave work and a certain group of contacts, and went on to college, where I made new friends. But, in fact I brought a lot of my network with me into Trinity and vice-versa. Some of them are married, and I know that they met each other through me. They all deny it now of course, because they think I am looking for money off them. I know I can name couples who met through the Ballymun — Ballyfermot — Trinity nexus.

When I was working for three years in advertising, I had a fairly okay job, but I wanted to go into the other area of advertising, the more lucrative end, which was accounting executive. And I came to the conclusion that I wasn't going to get into that unless I bettered myself. Looking at the executives who handle the accounts of companies, I saw that some of the guys doing it were totally incompetent and were regarded within the agency as frustrating to work with. They just couldn't manage anything. I was saying to myself at one stage, what have these guys got that I haven't? And one thing they did have was a network of contacts. They went to particular schools, and they had the people they went to school with, who were working in the companies that were handling the accounts. You know what I mean; they had played rugby together.

Defining Middle Class

As in anybody else's life, evolutions do occur, but what I don't accept is that changes affect my perception of the world. I am still as angry about unemployment and poverty as I was when I was eighteen. I still have the same perception of the world. To say you are middle-class is saying you now have a car, or you now have a mortgage. I have no choice because, I can't get a house from the Corpo. If that's the guideline that people are using to define middle class, well then it is a very narrow one. My politics, if anything, have become more radical. I don't disown particular causes; the only thing I would do now is be conscious of my job. I have a different job now. I do not and cannot disown other people's experience, their experience is as valid as mine.

I don't think I am middle class, I don't see that I am. On paper, perhaps, but it depends which guidelines you use. It is a statistical thing but you can't measure middle class. You can count the number of mortgage-holders in the country. Since I am one of them, I would be considered middle-class. But in terms of net work, I mean deep network in terms of family — my roots are working-class.

Health and Education

The main advantage of a middle-class upbringing would be health. The fact that middle-class people are healthier than working- class people is a huge thing in my head. Beginning with nutrition, teeth braces when you are kids, oranges and rubex and all that carry-on. Middle-class kids are healthier, and that is why they are good on a rugby pitch. Working-class kids are not as robust. They make better soccer players than rugby players. I am very conscious of my health, and looking after my health.

And I've become more conscious of music. There was always a radio in our house, it was a big feature. I think I've become more conscious of good food, or my taste buds have. Again I don't know whether those gains are propelled by age, class, culture or lifestyle.

I don't perceive myself as belonging to any social class. Maybe I would see myself belonging to the working-class because I don't have deep contacts in any other group in terms of people. I am not very class-conscious.

I've observed that people, whether middle-class or working-class, can be equally unhappy. I think that middle-class people are more private, whereas working-class people would be much more sociable. But the major differences would be in terms of health and education and choice and chance.

My politics is about more equal distribution of wealth, life, chances etc. Unlike John Major, for example, I do believe high taxes are justified if you are talking about good health services open to everybody. I do believe in an extra five pence in the pound. I have no objection whatsoever to a large proportion of my income going to the health services or to the Social Welfare. I do have a nasty feeling about people who have a lot more wealth than I could ever have, or even aspire to, and not paying their fair share and getting away with it for various reasons. I think the health service should be absolutely free. I also believe that everybody should have the service that is offered by the Blackrock Clinic to people who can pay. Everybody should have the facilities that are offered by the highest fee-paying school. I am not against the Blackrock Clinic, I just feel that everyone should have the same facility, but unfortunately they haven't.

What Politics Is About

My politics would be characterised as being Left. There is no reason for the existence of government or state other than to do good. There is no other legitimate reason. This has been well argued and established. The job of this state is to help those who are less well off, to help those who are falling below the average in whatever society. That is the purpose and reason for the existence of the state. The existence of the state is not in terms

71

of law and order versus anarchy. The only reason the state has for its existence is to do good for people.

It is very difficult for somebody to win a debate between fighting for more tooth brushes for children and taking money away from powerful multi-national companies. That is an old contest. It is an old contest in terms of the pressure the government will come under. The multinationals will tell them to get stuffed. The political party that does actually stand up for the toothbrush rather than the multi-national company and is prepared to face down the most powerful is the type of political party I would be interested in.

It is the same in all the media; the middle classes are more represented. When there is a mortgage increase of a half percent, that is the lead story in the newspaper. But if somebody's social welfare was cut, it would not necessarily be the lead story. If mortgages went up as much as bread sometimes goes up, every newspaper in the country would be calling for people to be on the streets. But bread means much more to working-class people than mortgages do. Mortgages always get greater coverage, greater analysis.

Why does every radio station, every television station, give out the FT100 and all this carry on? RTE does it and so do all the stations. What relevance has the FT100 got to the vast majority of people in this country? It would mean more to people if they gave statistics like: there were 94 houses allocated in Ireland to-day, or there was so many more children born. Real statistics. That is all meaningless to people. It effects one or two. People will come back and argue that it is a fact of the economy, and that may be, but it doesn't have a day-to-day effect on people.

Listen to the advertisements. They presume a nuclear family of two and two — two parents and two children. They presume you drive to the supermarket, whereas in fact more people in this country pull the two-wheel, tartan shopping trollies. There are more of them pulled to the supermarket than there are cars in this country, and yet you would never hear anyone on radio saying "now when you are putting your food in the trolley...". They say "next time drive to the supermarket". The presumption is that you have a car, that your family is stable enough, that both of you go shopping together, one of the kids will sit up and the other will walk around. A whole view of the world is given to you and it's a middle-class view. Legitimate for a lot of people, but not legitimate for everybody. Then the working-class image, is of a character and usually a Dubliner with an accent similar to my own. " Oh I heard this, what gets me about Jack Charlton is why doesn't he put O'Leary at the back," you know that stupid whatever it is called, easy slices or something like that. It is just absolute rubbish. If you see an add on television, everyone sits down for a meal together. They even sit down for breakfast together! That is totally foreign to me. It is a middle-class view of the world, because they are trying to sell to middle-class people.

Banned from Doing Ads

I am banned from doing adverts because my accent is so identifiable. I don't think that has happened anywhere at my level in RTE before. They ban me from a source of income. The reason that my accent stands out is the difference. It is not because of the nature of my accent, it is the difference. I am very identifiable, whereas other accents on the station are not. No one can tell where they are from or what type of background. People say I have a Dublin accent, but I don't. I have a Dublin working-class accent. That is the difference. There are as many accents in Dublin as there are in any other part of the country. I get comments now and then, comments like "A working-class Dublin accent does not represent Ireland". That's true, but neither does a mid-Atlantic accent. That is the answer to that. I am as much a representative as any other accent. I see that as a class thing, just snobbishness. People say: "I am disappointed in what my kids did and I hear this fellow on the radio and he is obviously from the working-class of Dublin, how did he get on so?" No one else is slagged over their accent, and there is a difference between accents and diction.

I am on the Gay Byrne show and I do a particular type of thing which has a particular listenership and then during the summer I fill in for the three months. You wouldn't want to over-estimate it. I know we have a huge listenership in terms of radio, it has a great penetration in Ireland. I came along at a time of internal competition from other RTE stations, and external competition from twenty other stations around the country. They targetted the programme I was working on. We held amazingly, I think. Gay Byrne has held on to his audience. In that new environment of twenty-one competitors, we have actually increased our audience in certain segments — like Dublin, and a younger age group.

I have a certain network of contacts that other people don't have, and we all use our network of contacts no matter where we are. I don't believe in a conspiracy theory either. When I say I want to use someone from Ballymun on the panel, the response is, what kind of person? are they good yappers? because this is radio. There is no conspiracy in here to keep out the working class. If there is any conspiracy it is the conspiracy of our own upbringing.

MICK RAFFERTY

A Family of Dockers

Mick Rafferty was born in Fitzgibbon Street, Dublin, where the family of six lived in a one room tenement. They moved to the new estates of Ballyfermot (where a farmyard and corn field faced the family home) and then, in the early 1960s, to the tough dockland community of Sheriff Street. In the space of a generation he witnessed the collapse of the old inner city economy and its replacement by financial services and other forms of economic activity alien to the old inhabitants. Over the past decade he has been involved in such key inner-city events as the Gregory Deal and Concerned Parents, and has been director of The North Centre City Community Action Project and the Inner City Renewal Group. He lives in Ballybough in the North Inner City and has three children.

My father was a docker, my mother was from a family of dockers. My grandfather worked in the Hammond Lane foundry on the South side. Both my parents came from an old working-class area. My father from a place called Peterson's Lane, near where U2's Windmill Lane is. And my mother came from Moss Street, which is where Irish Life has built its new office block. So I would describe my background as working-class. To work on the docks you had to have skills, not that it was a craft or a trade. When my grandfather, who was a docker, was alive he had the button, which was the method by which dockers became permanent or were guaranteed work. I was born in Fitzwilliam Street and we moved out to Ballyfermot. My father hadn't got a button. He was a youngish man, in his thirties. For a good long time he would come into town, or he would go down to the docks, but he might not be picked. It meant that he could come home that night, and he might have to say to my mother that he had no money.

The First Tube of Toothpaste

I remember at the age of seven the first toothpaste coming into the house and we used it all in one night because I think we kept brushing our teeth. I remember the first tin of soup coming into the house. I can also remember — though I can only remember having to have it once — the distinct smell of food in Ballyfermot they used to call "penny dinners". They still call them "penny dinners", but they are probably about five bob now. There were no holidays. My mother use to have to pawn stuff. I remember often she used to have to walk in from Ballyfermot to town, and she would go to a pawn shop in Gardiner Street. It is an open question whether I had a happy childhood or not.

We were fed, but a bit like a lot of families to-day. There were lean days, where the dinner might have been a sausage and some potatoes shared between two people, plus bread, milk and an egg. One of the treats at Christmas was a sweet. If there was real money around there was a bottle of chef sauce, so that shows the food was extremely basic. However I am five foot ten and muscular, so I must have been well fed.

Let me place the period. It was in the fifties, a tough time. There was no work. My father couldn't say: fuck the docks! and go into another job. The alternative was emigration. Maybe they weren't as hungry as the thirties. I can't remember whether there was some sort of welfare system. I don't think there was. In our family at one time there were six children under the age of ten.

There were times that my father had paid the bus fare, gone in at seven o' clock in the morning, had not been picked and he had to come home penniless. Out in Ballyfermot there was a shop facing us and my mother used to have to get tick. But there was an obvious limit to that. You couldn't go three days in a row. The woman in there at one point said you are reaching a stage where you are not going to be able to pay me back. That is why Dublin working-class people have a very close bond, because they share the few bob they have.

A Toy at Christmas

There were cousins of ours whose father was an electrician and they had the first television, they had the first cineprojector. We were sleeping on very hard beds and at Christmas we would get one toy. But I don't think any of us resented that. A mate of mine who comes from a similar background, came in one Christmas and my kids' toys were just all over the place. And he looked at me and said: "when I was their age I used to just get a gun and a holster" and I said: "you actually got the holster?". It wasn't like that constantly; there was a time they got more work, and things would improve. To compensate for that, where I grew up in Ballyer, where I spent my childhood, it was a forest and the suburbs were only developing. So you had a lot of people, some from the country and the inner city, so you had a sort of mixed community of people who to an extent were just establishing themselves in a new frontier. Much more than in the city, this was one of the things as a child I noticed that in the country (Ballyer) the seasons played a really important part in the behaviour and what you played with. My kids live in the city and they go through some of the phases, but not with the same intensity. Now I am talking about chestnuts, bow and arrows. My children can have access to them easily, but it is not the same. I think also nowadays there are a lot more marketable toys or fads like Batman or Bart Simpson. There were no fads around earlier, because there wasn't the money. The things tended to be invented. There was always someone on the street who would come up with some bizarre idea.

You would almost have to hypnotise me to bring me back, but you asked me did I feel a sense of deprivation. No, I didn't. There were things I would have liked, but I didn't go into a tantrum because I didn't get them.

There were a couple of people on the road who worked and we had one neighbour whose father had a relatively good job. They were able to get lots of things; they had the first television in the street. Eventually when we got a television it was second-hand. We couldn't get a decent aerial, so the screen was all snowy, which was good in a way because a lot of radio was listened to.But you would be conscious of this that somebody up the road had T.V.

Da Gets the Button

At one stage my father set up a football team, and this brought him into contact with politicians. A couple of times he would go out to the house to collect a cheque for something and I remember being in one of the houses, I was astonished by the amount of objects there were.

I think that my parents wouldn't have had much aspiration for us. We all went to school. I never mitched. None of the kids had that sort of problem, so they obviously encouraged us to go to school. But once I came to fourteen, there was no push to go on. I just left school at fourteen and went back to tech, after a year of being out in the real world. I would imagine their main hope was that we survived and reached adolescence and then they would leave it to ourselves. My father was in the docks, and by that time he had the button, so he naturally tried to get his sons work on the docks, and he did. Just after the tech, before I got an apprenticeship, I worked on the docks with my other brother. It would have been my father's aspiration I think that one of us follow him, one or more. Today, of the dozen dockers that's left working on the B & I, one of them is my brother.

One of my sisters ended up in a sewing factory in Rutland Street and that was a very common thing. She made all the gear for the local disco dancers, in Sheriff Street and East Wall, all around there, and it is beautiful. Her daughter, because of the way she looked and danced, won a trip recently to America and a trip to Disneyland as well. My sister made a couple of wedding dresses and a couple of communion dresses. She has an amazing visual capacity. If you asked her to go and look at a wedding dress and cut it, she would make it without reference to a pattern.

The parents' expectation would have been very much related to what was available, rather than to what was possible. I also think that the inner city is the same. A lot of kids leave school at fourteen or fifteen. Psychologically some of them leave school much earlier. They never really go. It is the same pattern.

Now the outlets aren't there like when we were young. When we were fourteen, none of us had a problem finding work. Relatively low pay, but the work was there.

Who Can Think of Tomorrow?

The great weakness in the whole working-class thing is precisely a lack of serious planning. Few people realise that, in order to be something, you have got to be able to take certain steps. You have to suspend certain things, to make certain sacrifices, etc... Living for the day is about struggling to make ends meet, so that is an understandable factor. People cannot think about to-morrow. I would think that the greatest weakness is our refusal to be socially mobile. We are scared of it. And that is obviously a very strong thing. Maybe humour is a strength, but humour can be a defence against changing. It is comfortable not to change, it is comfortable to remain within your group, it is comfortable not to break out.

The working-class great strength is also its curse. Stuff like getting involved in things like the trade union movement and the whole socialist movement is good. If you didn't become streetwise pretty quick, you became street-sore.

Nancy Boys

Obviously I was conscious of what we used to call Nancy Boys, who went to different schools. It wasn't so noticeable in Ballyfermot, not to the same extent, because that was a very homogeneous area. But it was certainly noticeable in the city where you were living in a block of flats. I was particularly conscious of O'Connell's schools, because I was going to Lawrence

O' Toole's which was adjacent to the Sheriff Street area. I mean it was terrible when you think about it. You only basically got into O'Connell's from Lawrence O'Toole's, if you were clever and had a scholarship. The following is about the birth of my clear understanding of what class was about.

One of the first jobs I got was as a messenger boy in a chemist shop, I was only thirteen-and-a-half. I was just out of school, it was during the summer. My birthday is in September, so when I left school in June I was thirteen. The first job was going around town delivering for the chemist and that was very strange. This was the first time that class struck me. I was on a message with my bike and I was actually coming around where I am living now, at the top of the road where I am living (cottages) and I know now it must have been about quarter past twelve because that is when the O' Connell boys had their break. (I know that now because my kids are going to O' Connell's). They stopped the bike, the package was in the front. Well I had to slow up. One of them took the package out and they started kicking it at each other. I don't think that I pleaded with them, it was sort of a combination of pleading and being angry. I eventually got it back. The boys going to O'Connells at that stage would have been much richer and more affluent than those going now. The whole structure of the inner city has changed; there has been further movement out. But you still get parents who live on the outskirts, as far away as Ashbourne, bringing their kids into O' Connell's. But at that stage it would have been a very small percentage of working-class kids going. Here I was, thirteen-and-a-half on a messenger boy's bike, and here were these older than me, fifteen or sixteen, going to secondary, and they were humiliating me and it was a telling encounter.

New Worlds

I mean there wasn't that much contact between my family and any sort of middle class, not that I can remember. The nearest thing coming to what I would have considered to be middle class would have been an uncle that had a steady job or something like that, but then again, when I think about it, up to the age of fifteen, there was relatively little contact outside.

Later on by my mid teens I deliberately went out to cultivate relationships with people who were thinking and writing and were generally doing different things from what I was used to. It was in true working-class groups like the Connolly Youth movement or the youth section of the Irish communist organisation where you tended to get middle-class people who would then introduce you to their world. But they were very exclusive worlds.

Television was only coming in, you didn't know an awful lot of what was going on. There was a great sense of intimidation as well about it. Even now I see kids around this area that if you asked them to go across to Grafton Street to Brown Thomas they would be very reluctant because they feel alien.

Also somebody said to me very recently where did you get that accent? I said: what accent are you talking about? I don't have an accent. What they confuse, I presume, is an ability to articulate with having an accent. Once you begin to think more globally and analytically, I suppose that you are immediately not one of the gang anymore because you have broken out of it. There is some vertical lift-off from that point. It is not social mobility. You are not someone who has broken out of the gang and got into the civil service for a job, and ten or fifteen years down the road has lost contact with everybody. A few of us were committed to sticking with work within a particular area, so its different from social mobility.

The Code of the Middle Class

As a kid I certainly got the impression that middle-class people lived richer lives and they had a lot more objects, but the kids particularly were much more pampered. They didn't take as many risks, so to some extent therefore didn't have as much fun. They had to conform to a code, much stricter than ours and this perversely was the punishment for all these objects. I suppose this is true, that the reward for us not having so many objects was that we had more fun. Also maybe they lived under a much stricter regime. A child growing up is in a largely non-thinking, non-analytical mode of growth. You don't think, you just experience things and accept everything as given. You don't ask why? Unless you say why can't I have that? And then you put pressure on your parents.

I don't know why this memory stayed: I was jumping from a wall over to the side, and I had to take certain risks. So I jumped, and there were two students, and they were amazed at this. I suddenly looked and said: you mean you don't jump like that? I think if I came across middle-class people as a kid, I felt that I must impress them. There was a sense of seeking their approval, because I felt somehow or other, it was important that they should be on my side. Again I changed very quickly to the opposite, and now of latter years I am coming back and saying I want to be your partner.

The Religious Phase

I went through a period of being quite religious, which pleased my mother. I went to mass and stuff like that. But strange enough she didn't push me to become an altar boy or anything, which I think I would have if I got a push. I think there was a great lack of confidence in me then. My da was active in trade unions. I think again his sense was of a fixed system that was accepted. I don't think that my father analysed the relationship between him as a docker and the employer in any market sense as a particular relationship or a particular moment in time. That was a fixed relationship and you tried to negotiate the best deal.

At school, there is a sort of acceptance about what is going on. When I started working there were a couple of tradesmen a bit more articulate, and it was a different environment, and it was really through that period that I became conscious not only of classes but also of the role of trade unions. No one brought me along. I still saw what was going on in Christian terms, even when I did begin to formulate it.

We counted our blessings, because we had moved from a one-bedroom flat in Fitzgibbon Street, sharing a bathroom or a toilet with the rest of the tenants. My father was involved in trade unions in the Marine Port and had been involved in a couple of strikes, so I was obviously conscious that we were working-class. But there wasn't really a socialist tradition in my family; I didn't hear words like working-class or ruling class or any sort of analysis.

Nationalism, Not Class

I suppose there was a bit more consciousness about nationality, in the fifties, and in school again the concentration was on nationalism rather than class. So that even in an area like Sheriff Street, when we were going to the Christian Brothers school in Seville Place, there was a definite concentration on all men, all women being equal in the sight of God, and that circumstances didn't matter, and in fact there was even an implication that if you were poor and hadn't got all the material goods there was less temptation, so therefore it was a good thing. That was the message. Part of the Christian Brother thing was that we should really pray for rich people, in the sense that Christ had said that the poor will always be with us. What they didn't explore (and it took me a while to understand the meaning of) was the whole thing about the camel getting through the eye of a needle. They never explored that sort of stuff. My real understanding of class started when I had to go to work in that little period I mentioned earlier, between fourteen and fifteen, when I could quite clearly see the inequalities of opportunity that were there. I saw that some people were destined to end up labourers, and lead relatively unhappy lives, in the sense that they were always struggling. And then you had tradesmen, who were a little bit better off, and then you had a managerial class, then you had the owners. People liked me, and I tried to ingratiate myself into those people who I saw were different and who had resources, because I thought that they were more powerful. It wasn't until I was about sixteen, when I started an apprenticeship with Dublin Corporation, that I began to meet people — electricians who were connected with the socialist movement. Then I joined the Connolly Youth Movement and began to read. That was my university. I got a clear marxist analysis of class centered on one's own real situation. I got to understand the material base of my own family. I realised things don't depend on God's will, that it is men who make decisions, and that this society is one particular type of society in a history of class struggle. That was a big leap.

Crossing Class Barriers

Yeah, I think both of my parents were extremely diffident. That is the word. And I inherited their attitude. I can still see it now, even in my kids, who tend to avoid coming in contact with people outside of their own class. I can never remember my mother or father being able to cross class barriers the way I can. For them their class was an unspoken weakness. It was due to a lack of education, an accent, and to some extent poverty. To me it was great to flaunt your class. But to them it was something to hide.

Out of the six children, I was the only one who completed second level education and then went on to serve my time and finish. The rest remained semi-skilled and I became a skilled tradesman. I mentioned earlier about my sister being a seamstress but she doesn't work at that; she cleans offices, because of the collapse of the clothing industry. My eldest brother up until recently worked down at the docks in a metal factory. But now it is cheaper to import the stuff from England. So he lost his job after fifteen years. Through connections of mine, he ended up working in the theatre; first in the Rocky Horror Show and then in a couple of other shows like the German Hamlet and the Japanese Macbeth. He is presently working in the Abbey on a casual basis. He had no previous experience of theatre, but he is recognised as a great stage hand and he now almost has a managerial role. The other brother continued on and took my father's tradition at the docks, and the one other brother works in a builders and again it was a mate of mine, who is quite well off, gave him that job.

Community Projects

As for me, my social status now is that I am a manager of a community project and I have a number of individual projects going. I am emloyed by an number of projects in this area; most of the projects are represented on my management board, and I helped create that situation through years of work. I am responsible for running the programme. This means I have to have relationships with groups from Cork to Belfast, and from Derry to Wexford. Paradoxically, after all these years we come to recognise in the community groups that we have to have areas of partnerships with the private sector, with the middle class if you like, and we are consciously seeking ways in which that can be done. In a sense it is the private sector, the rich, who destroy this area both by suddenly moving out traditional factories (as in the case of my brother) and for the rest of the people living in this area, because essentially the people who controlled the wealth, who controlled the means of production, moved out and the new industries coming in (or the new financial services coming in) don't want local people because of class prejudices. I find myself trying to bridge some of those gaps, which is a strange position to be in. The best way that I could put what it is that I do is retain street credibility, but have gravitas. Be accepted by the private sector, but this time not with diffidence but as a partner. In a sense the bosses also realise that it is in their interest to solve some of the social problems that are around.

During my late teens, I had progressed in the Connolly Youth movement into different organizations, all on the Left, so by the end of the sixties I had been involved in a number of issues — the Housing Action Committees, the Vietnam war issues, the initial EEC referendums, the PR referendum. I was a working-class guy with a political consciousness, but still with a healthy attitude to fashion and to women.

At that time I was a bit scared of middle-class women, even though the latter group that I became involved in, the ICO (the Irish Communist Organisation), tended to attract students, whereas the CYM tended to attract working-class guys.

A Character in Search of an Author

By the end of the sixties, it began to seem very abstract to me, in that there was this notion about class and yet you could quite clearly see, there wasn't the class consciousness there, you know there was maybe group consciousness or community stuff. So I left some of those. I left that sort of era, and after some time in England, I came back and began to live in flats around Dublin and began to get involved in the literary side. A couple of us still got involved in running a paper called The Agitator which had been published in the sixties by Denis Denny. He was the lad who became famous because he was jailed that time he had squatted in a house. We continued on that, myself and another couple of guys, both from the city and from Ballyfermot but when I look back the unemployment figures at that stage were perhaps 90,000 and they are nearly three times that now.

I was living up in Mount Street and there were three people that I knew, that I quite enjoyed being with. Neil Jordan lived around the corner. And Des Hogan. A whole lot of people who were themselves on the verge of some sort of career. At that stage I had finished my time and I was freelancing. An Australian living in Dublin called Jim Ryan, came up to the flat and said he had heard about me from somebody down in Sheriff Street and that he wanted to know if I would get involved in the Sheriff Street tenants organisation. This was quite strange. He was involved in a group called the Dublin Tutorial group which essentially was a group of middle-class people who brought kids from Sheriff Street to Liberty hall and gave them classes in art, drama and basic literacy and they were known as the Tutorial group. That particular group was the beginning of an approach to community development which was breaking away from the old youth club-orientated thing. There were clubs around at that time — the Bru Lorcan, the Belvedere's — but a lot of those clubs had very little involvement in the community. They were just dealing with the kids and that was it. Dealing with the community issues, you would have the St. Vincent De Paul or the nuns. This was the first time that I had really come across it. It came at a very convenient time because I was coming out of that class party approach. I was like a character in search of an author. I was looking for context. I wasn't involved in the trade union movement at this stage, because I wasn't really working. I wasn't connected. I was involved in a number of issues, but there was no context for it. It was really from that eventually I went down and got involved in the tenants organizations and began to enjoy it. I began to introduce ideas, began to organise festivals down in Sheriff Street, began to be seen as an important leader there, began to lead protests, began to come up with plans for development and got a lot more people involved and that lasted a while. Then we made a film called "It is a hard old station". Some of the people who made that, people like Tessi MacMahon, are still involved and Tessi is still living in Sheriff Street. That was in 1973. I went back to work as an electrician and worked out in Dun Laoghaire, so that I became involved in trade unionism again. I became a shop steward out there, I enjoyed it, I was out of the stress for a while. All that community stuff can become very stressful.

A Squat in Sherrif Street

I got married to a woman from Brigid's Gardens down in Sheriff Street, Ann Burke, and we were living in North Great George's Street, so I wasn't involved really with that sort of community stuff. I would go in and out. We found she was pregnant after about a year. It was Michael Smith, the poet, that I was friendly with at the time, (I think I was doing some work with him), he said, why don't you squat down in Sherriff Street? We did, myself and Ann. We went down to see some of the flats. Even at that stage the Corporation was letting out to families that were not desirable in the area. So the consequences of that housing policy can be seen now, in that there are quite a few undesirables down there that don't belong to that community. It was only people within the area who would want to live there, other than people who were on the very last rung, who had probably already been evicted from a number of areas. They would have been put into an area that had enough problems of its own. One way of stopping that, was that young couples from the area were encouraged to squat. So here I was back inside Sheriff Street, but it wasn't to last that long really.

One night in 1976 Tony Gregory and Fergus, came up and said that they had got money from Combat Poverty to run this programme and that it was all the things that we had set out to do, but now we had money. They wanted me to apply for the job, so I had to think about it because I wasn't sure whether or not I wanted to get back in. I could now have a career as a electrician. After the experience of working out in Dun Laoghaire perhaps I could set up on my own, and just maintain the involvement in the trade unions and go that direction. But I applied for the job, and I got it. I became director of this community project, The North Centre City Community Action Project. I have seen people come and go, who stayed in a place for about a year and a half and then moved off. But a lot of this sort of stuff we are talking about is more than a job for us.

Looking for Security

I was very conscious of the possibility of social mobility, of moving completely out, but I think once I made a decision to be employed the way I am at the moment, that is through community groups. I think I also made a decision to go with what we were doing as long as possible, I don't want to change my class but I would certainly like to have more income and I certainly would like to be more secure.

Real class is something else. It is about heritage, it is about a certain ethos, it is about a whole set of factors which money in itself doesn't bestow upon you. It is not the money, the resources, the disposable income, that necessarily makes for a different class. I think it is possible to accumulate money and still remain within the one class. It would depend on the way you are making the money. You wouldn't be involved in enterprise, except maybe through a co-op, and the co-op itself rewards it's members. But you always remain within your class. You do different things with your money. You write a book or you make a film. But psychologically or sociologically you are still relating much more to your origins and to your identity. And the relationship with the others is simply a business relationship. Now ideally that is the one for me, because I don't like lots of middle-class people. I mean I just don't like them as a class. I get on well with a lot of individuals, but I don't like the sort of expectations that they place on people, and I don't like their concern with comparing their material positions all the time and references all the time to what they have and what they don't have. I have seen couples who have set off to do different things, different middle-class things like not sending their kids to the local school but some other school, like multi-domination schools which I fully support but I have seen them after a while resort back to more traditional ways.

"Where You Will End Up"

There are two types of people who would become conscious of their background. I mean there is the sort of hard core working-class guy who becomes a kind of caricature in that he couldn't give a bollocks about anything. He cultivates a sort of a wit and an accent, but essentially could end up pretty pathetic because he (she) becomes stereotyped. He can't be socially mobile. He is essentially a clown. He is no threat to anybody.

And the other is a very talented, perhaps creative person. I remember hearing this story; there was a group of students, women from a very high-class secondary school brought on a visit to Jervis Street where there is a FÁS training course. It looks good, so one of the managers showed the girls around with the nun and when the nun was on the way out she said to the girls on the stairs, "Now girls if you don't study hard this is where you will end up." That to me reveals a real attitude to work, that if you don't study hard you won't get into daddy's bank or whatever, you would end up being a worker. You instil the fear of social downward mobility into them. Whereas I mean the ideal that I would love is that some of our people, that some of the people that live here, can be given an opportunity to break out of the class position that they are in because there is nothing romantic about living in Sheriff Street, in an area with eighty-per-cent unemployed. That is why we are here, to improve the situation, to give people a greater sense of money. There is nothing sadder than having to see somebody from a working-class background having to change their accent, having to put on a false air about themselves. In other words they actually become more right-wing in lots of ways. They begin to adopt racist attitudes, and you can see it is because they want to become middle-class. They are lost. That is a terrible price for a human being to pay simply to belong to a class which in the end will reject him anyway.

Relationships

My closest friends are community workers/artists. I drink, and socialise in either Hill 16 or the Sunset. I try to avoid going across to the southside. This job and my involvement in politics with Tony Gregory necessitates meeting people from all the different sectors. One of the people I have seen very recently is Mark Healy Hutchinson. He is the ex-director of Bank of Ireland, and is now involved in, (for want of a better word) Community Enterprise. I see this man learning that all his prior conceptions about what you could do are beginning to change. He initially thought that maybe we were negative, but he is beginning to see the obstacles that are there. So what I am saying is that sometimes they are operating mutually, exclusive circles that never overlap. There are a lot people like Mark Kavanagh or even Paul Mc Guinness, with whom I have some sort of relationship. I mean I know them, and both of them would have funded some parts of our programmes. It is a close corporate relationship almost, which is what we would want, like the professional relationship, based on the fact that we are operating in a particular sector and they are operating in another.

Recently I met this lad who is quite influential in the private sector. We want to raise funds, to acquire property, to develop a decent resource centre which is missing in this area. I asked him the same question: "Well, what do you think is an obstacle?" Now I am talking from the point of view of the working-class activist but he said, "well you know you would be associated with Gregory, and Gregory moans against everything." I don't think he does but the image is of these angry left-wingers who are like wolves ready to pounce on anybody who speaks other than with an north-inner-city accent, and that is absolutely not true. But that is what he said. He said like when I sit down and talk to you, you can be very witty, funny and charming. And he said that is the problem. These personal contacts break down prejudices. Try to arrange a series of meetings in which we can show them our attitudes and our way of work, that it is a different type of work, that it is not a threat to them, it's constructive. The other thing, from the point of view of an ordinary worker, I mean the main barrier is images but images are prejudices, if you give a certain address, people will assume the worst about you. But there are some noble exceptions to that. I mean people who will take you at face value. I think they are rare but they are there. I remember we went over to London in a group; John Kane and Seannie Lamb and myself and a lovely middle-class woman — an architect. At times she thought that the way we were going on, she would actually feel there was going to be a fight. Wearing your heart a bit more on your sleeve can become a barrier, because a lot of people don't want to have to deal with emotions.

The White Socks Story

The famous story about the socks, I think it is a pretty classical example of that whole area of the message that you give out that can totally define your whole life. This guy actually rang up I think it was the Pat Kenny or the Gerry Ryan show and he said: I am from a semi-upper-working-class background, but I have this job in a recruitment agency and we advertised for these jobs and we got thousands of applications, so even after we went through the CV's, there were still hundreds of people that were eligible for the job. So we started doing group stuff trying to eliminate, meeting about thirty of them. And we were going to go from group to individual, to weed out. The boss called us in and said, this process is taking too long, it is costing us a lot of money, we have only got a certain amount of budget to do this, you have to quicken up the process. And they said how? He said there is only one way to do that, to go through each individual and to eliminate anybody wearing white socks. White socks come from poor backgrounds, and that is not the person we want for the job. That is remarkable, isn't it? And it is true. Bouncers look down and say no you are not getting in because you are wearing white socks. You asked what are the obstacles? White socks are a major obstacle.

ALICE TAYLOR

Culchie

Alice Taylor grew up in a rural Ireland that was still basking in the glow of oil lamps and where farm work and transport was still carried out by horses. These experiences became the subject for her first two books, the best-selling To School Through the Fields and Quench the Lamp. After leaving secondary school she worked in the Civil Service as a telephonist. She married in the early sixties and moved to the village of Innishannon. Her experience of life and changes there formed the basis of The Village. She is now one of Ireland's most popular authors.

We never knew the word "culchie", because we lived in a whole culchie culture. I remember a cousin coming from Dublin and someone calling him a Dublin jackeen and that was the first time I heard of it. But the funny thing is that he didn't react by calling us culchies. We didn't feel that we were culchies because we didn't know the difference between a culchie and a Dublin jackeen. I suppose the difference we saw was the differences from the people in the town. Dublin and Cork City would be too far away; we compared ourselves to those in the local town. I remember there were people who wore polished shoes everyday.

People with Polished Shoes

We walked to school across the field and there was mud on everything. Everything around the farm yard was naturally a bit muddy and it carried in all over the place. One thing I remember thinking was that there were people that actually had their shoes polished all day and everyday, and people that didn't have to get their hands muddy when they were working.

I suppose our farm originally would have been the biggest farm at that time, but it was divided up when different members of the family got married. Two other farms had originally been part of our farm. In a sense that made us a kernel of the town land. We felt very much that. My father felt that if anybody was on their own, or anybody wasn't able to cope, he should assume responsibility for them. I remember there was one old lady who lived near us on her own and when the snow was there he would visit her everyday and make sure she had milk or the messages. And it was no bother to him to send us, walking into town, three miles, to get something she needed and walk out again. You felt that if other people had problems they were your problems as well. I think what that did afterwards to me is that it made me feel almost responsible for other people's problems.

The food was very simple. It all came off the farm, and there was no such thing as buying lemonade or cakes or anything like that. Our own wheat would have been the flour; we would have killed our own pig, that would have been meat; all the potatoes, vegetables, and eggs were our own. We made our own butter. Afterwards that came from the creamery. So everything came off the farm. There wasn't a thing from outside that could have any effect on us. The only two things that we bought were a gallon of paraffin oil for the lamps and the battery for the radio. Candles were counted as second-rate lighting. The lamp in the kitchen was the thing, so it was a terrible thing if you ran out of oil. You would have to walk across to the neighbours for a gallon of oil if you were stuck. My father had to have the radio going. If the battery ran out, it was a pure disaster. I mean my children today have the radios roaring all over the house. But then the radio was turned on, for the news, for different plays on Radio Eireann and different plays on BBC. My mother, if she heard something which she didn't think a hundred percent, she would turn it of. So we listened to the radio a lot.

"Enough to Rear Another Family"

There was no such thing as waste and anything that was left over after any of the meals would feed the hens, the cats, dogs and the pigs, everything was used up. I suppose that would be still with me, this sense of not to waste things. My father used to say: "there is enough thrown out in this house than would rear another family". I occasionally say to my children: how can you waste that when half the world is starving? And they finish it for me. And I say: that is my father talking now. I mean when he used to say that at home long ago, I would say: how could he mean that? I would say: that is ridiculous. And here I am saying the same thing now! I am very conscious of wasting things. We were reared to that.

A Goose at Christmas

There was plenty of everything, but none of the luxuries. You always brought something if you were visiting the neighbours (well not visiting the neighbours nearby, you ran in and out of those houses) but if you went visiting cousins who lived far away from home you would always bring something with you. I remember in turn Auntie Molly would visit us and she would always bring a cake and huge bags of apples. I remember my mother had a sister living in town, and every Sunday morning my mother took her a big brown cake and two big whiskey bottles full of milk. We would have tea in her house after Mass, and she would have lovely home-made apple tarts. It was almost as if it was an exchange. My mother used to always say if you are going to go visit don't go with your two hands hanging to you. And still if somebody came to visit me and brought a pot of homemade jam, I would just love it. My father had married cousins who lived in town. At Christmas he would take every one of them a bag of potatoes off the farm. My mother would kill seven or eight geese and they would always be from the farm, and then they would send something to my mother. It was an exchange. It wasn't thought of as a Christmas present. We didn't buy to give it; we had it. We gave of what we had. And I can remember that the pony and cart would go to town for Christmas simply to take the potatoes and things.

Dressing Up

The clothes situation was very limited because I was the youngest of five girls so I was wearing the hand-me-downs and very seldom you would have something new bought and when you did have by God it really was something. I can always remember getting my first pair of sandals, and walking up and down the counter when we fitted them on. But most days it was hand-me-down clothes. And we had Sunday clothes, clothes that you would put on going to mass and then hung in the wardrobe from Sunday to Sunday. When you came home from mass they were taken off. The clothes for going to school and going around the yard were totally different. They were too big and too loose and they were belonging to someone else.

There was no one well-dressed as such. Maybe the teacher's children were a bit better dressed than the rest of us, but they came from the town. They came out with the teacher so they didn't come across the fields and weren't all mud when they arrived. All the rest of us did. We totally outnumbered them.

Parcels from America

I remember we used to get parcels from America. That was a big thing at that time. I remember I had a godmother in America and she would send parcels and there were clothes, lovely colours and everything. The ones that went to America were very good to the people at home. Now no money came to our house, but they did send clothes. But I would say in a lot of houses money did come. I would say rural Ireland owed a lot to the people that went away. When they did come home they were given a great reception and a good time, because they deserved it.

I used to love putting on the Sunday clothes. You see we got all cleaned up and washed for Sunday and the new clothes went on and we went to town and you saw people that you assumed were like this everyday, which they probably were. That was the big difference in us alright, that we saw the town people as different.

Learning Bits and Pieces

I don't know whether my parents were very specific about getting a job. We went to a secondary school which opened in the town. It was assumed that at some stage you would get a job, but of course there was no great difficulty in getting a job at that time. It was assumed that when you had your Leaving done you did an entrance exam for the bank, the civil service, the county council or something and the chances were that you would fall into something. I don't know whether there was much unemployment. That would have been in the late fifties/early sixties. There wasn't, you see. When I had my Leaving done, I went to do domestic science for a year and I remember protesting to my mother that it was a waste of time. But she said you will go back there and you will learn something that will be of benefit to you. My mother had always great time for nuns. Now even though I did protest about going, I did learn a lot that was of benefit afterwards, different little bits and pieces. And when I came out of it I kind of thought: I wonder will I ever use this? But when I got married I did actually, when I ran a guest house.

I did the civil service exam and I was called and I became a telephonist there. I didn't think that is what I wanted to do. I took it because it turned up, and I didn't question it. And when I went there I enjoyed it. It was my first time away from home. I went to stay with a lady who lived on her own and I was quite happy there. I was on my own two feet, it was up to me to look after myself. There was six of us. There was no question of going to university, because at that time you paid for university and there was no question of paying for that many. I felt they have done what they can for me now. I have been educated and I have my job and it is up to me to look after myself and to be self-sufficient. I mean the wages weren't great but I wouldn't dream of sending home for money because I felt that they had kept their end and that I should keep mine. As well as that, maybe it was drummed into us growing up that you looked after yourself and you didn't expect anyone else to pick up the pieces after you.

Jobs on the Farm

On the farm there were always jobs to be done, the eggs had to be brought in, the calves had to be brought in, the cows had to be milked. Different jobs every day, and everybody had their own jobs, and you were responsible for them. If you brought in the eggs, you didn't leave a couple so that the greyhounds came and ate them afterwards. It was all necessary to keep the show on the road, so that everybody contributed their own share even though I, being the youngest, opted out more than any of the others. But at the same time I remember even when we were going to school, it was our job to change all the beds, wash down the stairs, polish them, clean out the kitchen. It was our job, and we didn't question it. This sense of doing what had to be done was with you and if you didn't do it, it would have been somebody else who would have had to do it, so you did your part.

You had to pull your weight. My mother was very easy-going. She didn't say "do this" or "do that" or she wasn't rigid in any way. We took it upon ourselves, being five girls in the one house. My eldest sister took over and allocated responsibility down and my mother left us at it. She was busy too. That time on a farm, the farmer ran the farm but the wife ran the farmyard. She was responsible for the turkeys, the hens, and the calves. The women looked after the baby animals, as well as other things, so she was very busy outside. My mother milked the cows every morning. In a way the farmers' wives were the first of the working wives. I think looking back it brought a great sense of togetherness in the sense that we all pulled in the one direction to keep the thing going. There was plenty to eat, which we got from the farm. The clothing was adequate, the cloth was bought in the local shops and the clothes were made up with the dressmaker, everything was done locally.

Wary of Kisses

My mother was very quiet. I never remember her losing her temper and she wouldn't cry easily. When my brother died, I remember my mother crying that day and I was shattered by it. She was a very easy person and you always felt around my mother that it was almost like being in a calm sea. She never would go into highs of anger, or highs of depression, or highs of love, or highs of anything. It was just serenity round her. You felt safe with my mother. She was very even. My father was totally different. He would lose his temper easily and he would also do it with us and he would do it with the animals and he would flare up and then he would calm down as just fast. We children would fight and row with each other and afterwards we sometimes cried bitter tears. I think we expressed ourselves when we were happy because we would sing. I can remember that there was a lot of singing in the house. My brother, who was the oldest, was a lovely singer and he always sang at his work. Love wasn't expressed in words. You did it, rather than said it. I would say that it was incorporate. And I suppose it is still that way with me today. I would be a lot more impressed by what people would do than what they would say. I think it is very easy to tell someone you love them, it is only costing you words, But doing the thing for them, even to go out as far as the neighbours to help or to give them something rather than tell them how good they were. I remember there was this very posh cousin who used to come visiting, and she would come into the house and she would kiss my mother on the cheek. I didn't like her much anyway but when she went away I often felt it was a performance that we got, and as true as God to this day I am very wary of these people who kiss one another when they meet. I often wonder what to make of them. To me it has to be meant. With my sister now I would put my hands around her and kiss her, but that is because I love her.

I remember an uncle that lived back down the road from us. When the snow would come, he would visit to find out if we were alright. I remember us all getting the flu at some stage, and he would come to us on the horse. It was all horses at that time. Horses could get through the snow when you couldn't come any other way. Now he would no more have put his arms around my mother who is his sister and said I love you and what a wonderful sister and all that. But he would come to know if she was alright. That was the way it would have been done.

An Early Environmentalist

Up the hill in the village, back in the sixties, there was an old lady and she looked after the church and she owned a little sweet shop. She had a sister an invalid in a wheelchair. Now Ellie was over eighty, but she would go off with her sister in the wheelchair. She never said I have to do it or I should do it, But in her world you looked after your own, and you didn't even think about it. I would say it was just second nature, and I would say at that time on a farm, the animals were very much a responsibility so that maybe it transcended that you looked after anything that couldn't look after itself, like the horses. Now the horses are the next things to human beings in the animal kingdom and my father-in-law is very fond of horses and he had this thing about trees, about the landscape and caring for the environment. That time we never heard the word "environment" but if you cut down a tree he had a fit. There were always plenty of trees, he had this thing about looking after the earth and he was always talking about the balance of nature. If people upset the balance of nature he used to always say: "there is a terrible price to be paid". He was talking about that when we were children. We grew up listening to that — not wronging the land, but caring for it.

100

Wise People Running the World

I suppose the advantage of a rural upbringing was the space. There was great range for the imagination, because you had the fields to go out and entertain yourself in, you were near to nature with the birds, you had the farmyard and the fields you had great space. I think that was the big plus. That is sort of still inside my head and to me it is an extension of home. They were the pluses, and I think the fact that you were held responsible for yourself. There was no one else that would come tidying up after you.

I grew up thinking that there was an adult world that was far wiser than me. We were always told that, on our own farm we were fine, but out there somewhere — on the radio or BBC or RTE — there were wise people that could run the world very efficiently. Because we could run our corner, they were able to run their corner — the greater part of the world. We, as children, couldn't ever have the wisdom that they had. They were the greatest, they knew what they were doing. It took me a long time to realise that they didn't know what they were doing. Maybe we should have been made more aware that our wisdom was as good as their wisdom. I grew up for a long time thinking that the adult world knew everything and it was a long time before I realised they didn't.

Nobody was a Stranger

In the rural world there were no social barriers because we were all in the same boat. I often think that the people working on the farm, weren't working for us, they were working with us. They shared everything that we shared, they had the same hardships that we had. We had one old man that used to come to stay with us, he was a travelling farm worker. We were happy to treat him right, because he used to always say that he had great respect for people, no matter how contrary they were. The door was never locked, he would come in day or night, and he would go into the room at the end of the house. My brother used sleep in there, and he would come in and be there in the morning, He stayed as long as he liked, and went when he liked. I don't think he would survive in today's world because there isn't the same freedom of movement. You wouldn't let a stranger into your house now, down the country. He wasn't a stranger, but he must have been a stranger at some stage. The man who used to come to sweep the chimney would camp down at the bridge. He came every year, so everything formed a pattern.

The "itinerants" as they are called now, we used to call them "tinkers". They were the same. They came all the time. Then there was a lame woman, she used to come to my mother. God, they were great friends. They would compare notes about children and everything, and she came for years. There were no outsiders coming in as such; there was nothing to feel threatened by, because everybody knew everybody.

Outside Worlds

I suppose the fact that they shared our lives totally made us unaware that there was any great difference. Maybe I thought they had more fun. One used to play the piano (the melodeon, we called it) and he used to play it in our house and also back in his own home, and from that I used to think that they had more music and more fun. He worked in our house for years and years. He is retired now, but I still call into him when passing. He is a great friend and we talk about growing up. Because of the music I thought there was more fun in his house than there was in ours, since he took his music home with him, and we only had it when he was there with us. The local doctor would come into the house. He was from a different world and he had a different look about him. His hands were very fine and delicate. He just looked different, very clean, antiseptic, medical. Then I think there was a cousin of my father's coming here as a priest from London and he was a fine big tall man, and I said: gosh he is from a different world. He is out there meeting all types of people totally outside of our world even though his mother would have been born on our farm. Then there was a first cousin, a Franciscan. I had a picture of a holy world. I visualised him in long corridors in a monastery and people praying. Him with the profession of prayer, and the doctor with the profession of cure, and the priest keeping the world right in London, and they came from worlds outside my world. They were very different.

My grandmother used to come to visit us very seldom, and I used to think that she came from an old world. She had a sister, a grand aunt, who used to come also, and I used to think that her mind was away in a world before we came. Other people used to come home from America and they were very different. They were out there in a very colourful place.

Us and the "Help"

We worked in the farmyard, and did the same work the farm "help" did. I remember once a farm worker who used to come. He was very cranky, and he was holding forth, and my mother gave out to me for calling him a name because he was older, and people that were older than me deserved more respect. Anyone working on the farm was treated the same as ourselves. Often they weren't much older than the older ones of us, and we fought and argued with them, and they fought and argued with us about different things. There were no differences, and they slept in our bedrooms and we shared the jobs around the house. There was one neighbour with a large family. My father would give her part of the bacon and help her out. Everybody would know how much everybody else had, because you knew by their cows. They were there for everyone to see. And whether the potatoes got blight or whether the pig didn't make the price of the fair, everybody knew how everything was. It was very easy to know how many mouths people had to fill. If there was not enough, the fellow who had it would give it. That was the way it would work.

No Hidden Poverty

There was one house in particular where the thatch wasn't great and a leak used to come in. There was no such thing as hidden poverty, it was all out in the open. The only extra that anyone might have was if someone from America was sending home money. You noticed some people were better able to manage. Women worked very hard that time. They had great nerve. In a way now you think of the working wives and it is great how they are coping; but these were super-women before super-women were ever heard of.

Wet Days at School

We were very unquestioning when I think back on it. I mean it was always easy and we sailed along with it. We were very taken up by the blackberries in the summer and being able to go barefoot to school, and the interesting thing was the changing of the field and the rain going to school. And I can remember feeling cold. You would arrive in school and you would be soaking wet and you could take off your overcoat but you sat in your soaking wet clothes all day, and also there was a fierce draught under the door. I never got warm. I always associate school with being cold. We were cold for hours. It didn't get warm until about two o'clock, and anyway there were holes in the doors and the windows rattled. There was wind hopping through the place. You couldn't heat it. It was grand in the summer but in the winter if you arrived in on a cold wet morning, you would stay cold all day long.

I was aware that there was another world outside this, but it had no connection with what we were doing at the time. My father was always listening to the news and the BBC, and I would listen and I would just think: out there now, there is another world going on. Nowadays the whole of world activities are, in a sense, inside in our house. And as children grow up, they know of everything that is going on. But we didn't. We were totally absorbed in that world and we knew nothing, we heard it on the news but we were very far removed from anything that was going on outside.

Vision of a Fur Coat

Once I remember experiencing wealth. We were coming home from Mass one Sunday in the town, I can't remember what age I was but I remember standing in the street and this beautiful big car pulled up in front of a house. This lady came out of it with a gorgeous fur and beautiful hat, and I can always remember myself fixed in a trance, looking at her. She hit me like a ton of wood. And that evening I remember thinking what kind of a world does she come from? It was the first fur coat I had ever seen, and she was in total contrast to everything I had ever witnessed up to then. I remember that evening thinking about that woman and where did she come from. And how did this beautiful coat come to be. There had been a big transfix in my whole life, and she was in my head, and I almost felt that if I could accompany her that I could see into a different world. I remember thinking afterwards about her. She was from a different world to me. That was the first impact of meeting it in the flesh — the outside world! Whether she was home on holidays, or where she was coming from, I don't know, but she definitely wasn't a native of our place.

Unfamiliar Fields

I don't think I would like to live in a city. I like the village. You go out onto the street and you know you will meet somebody to have a chat with. There is great companionship in a village. And I can shop in the village. But I miss the fields, even though I am surrounded by them here, because you walk along the road. There is a difference between that and walking through fields. You can I suppose jump over and walk in the fields but you don't know the fields so they won't have the same feelings.

I would be more inside my own skin in the fields of my own farm than I would be anywhere else. Now I go into the woods, I would still have that sort of spiritual renewal or something inside in the wood, or out in the field, but there is something inside me that built up in childhood that still is reawakened by going into fields that I know, or into the woods, or even sitting and looking at the river. I like the village in the sense that there is a mixture of the community. I like that. I don't think that I would like to live in a housing estate, the people all around me would be of my own age group. I think it is nice to have a good mixture within the community and you have the farming community in on top of us as well. You have the clubs now in the village, all the different organizations. But inside of those organizations you could have anyone. You would have the farmers. You could have the village people, you could have the people working in Cork that are living here, you would have people from all different ways of life intermingled.

Silent Spaces in Between

I think if you grew up on a farm you got used to spending a lot of time on your own and I think you always keep that need inside of you. I like to be on my own a bit. I mean I would come home now from book signing and things, and I would shut the door and I would just sit here. Yes I need to withdraw and I think that is probably as a result of growing up where we spent a lot of time on our own. I mean even though there were six of us there you still spent a lot of time that you would live within your own imagination, your own head and I would still need that, you know, even though I like people and I like being with them.

A Vanishing World

There is a new attitude evolving for the people in rural Ireland It is very important that the people in the country should be aware that there is a quality of life that might be gone before we realise how valuable it is. We are at a cross roads where we could pull the old values, they were rooted actually in centuries of wisdom. In my generation people would say: it is terrible altogether that these wakes have been lost, a terrible way, no respect for the dead, and all this crack. And they would be bawling below in the parlours. I don't know about certain circumstances but there was a lot to be said for the old wakes and the old way of doing things. Now, the way life is lived, it is nearly moving too fast for the mind; and the mind is going nowhere. The old way gave people time to adjust. Maybe we could evolve back.

Getting a Husband

My mother was very adamant about not getting married young. I remember when I talked about getting married, I was only twenty and she said: you are far too young. But she was worried about whether it would work out alright. I think she was very tuned into the idea of marrying someone that you would be happy with, and that they would be happy with you. As mother used to say someone "suitable". She meant someone suitable in temperament. That they weren't going in a different direction to you. I always remember afterwards she used to say to me, I worried so much about you because you were so young and I thought God would you be able to handle a shop business after being reared on a farm. Afterwards she was laughing, God, she said, it worked out fine and you were grand. She was always very relieved, and she said afterwards, "I was so pleased about my five son-in-laws".

Turn Off The Telly

Closing down the small national schools was a mistake. If you take the young fellows out of the community and put them in a school far away, now they might end up "better educated" but there are a lot of different interpretations of what "better educated" means. We were fierce lucky here to have our school.

107

I think it would have been better for rural Ireland if the local schools had been kept because you have a focal point for the community and people are in their own environment. It is almost as if they were putting education before people. I think they should have put it parallel. Educate them in their own environment. I don't know if it is more economical. It probably costs as much to bus them to the other schools. I think one of the things the rural people themselves will have to do is to do their business in rural Ireland, not to be going into the cities to do it. They will have to support their own communities in order to survive. What is made locally is good, and we should support it and help ourselves because if we don't help ourselves we are going to go down the swanny. Growing your own vegetables, having your own hens, growing your own things — might not be economical. In one sense it might be cheaper to buy things from a supermarket. I think the fact of having your own and growing your own vegetables gives a meaning, a satisfaction, to people. I think we all have creativity in us.

We are very inclined to think that it is only actors and writers who have creativity. We have creativity for gardening, for baking, for knitting, for pottery. I think we should do things on our own, to appreciate the quality of life that is here. I think all children, my children, the children of the next generation will look back and say: we were the crowd who let rural Ireland slip out of Irish hands. We should appreciate what we have, and I think we should turn off the bloody television and go and talk to the neighbours. I think they are not probably alone in this in rural Ireland. We nearly know more of what is going on in New York than we do about what is going on next door. I think that there is a great need for just checking on people, and taking the time to talk to them. You hear about people dying and being found a week after. I know now what everybody says about rural villages that everybody knows everybody's business. So what? I think that is a great thing, because if you have a problem you have someone to help you. If you have the door locked and you are inside, nobody can help you and there isn't the back and forth between houses.

In the heel of the hunt there is nothing as comforting as another human being, someone to sit down and talk to. I find that great, you know, — someone to talk to, to cry to, why not get back into the way things were always? I would put a lot of emphasis on that, the human relationships in the community.

The young were leaving the land, and I know there is all economics about it, but we are inclined to think as well that there is nothing for them in rural Ireland. But maybe they would come back afterwards and say there was more there than we saw. It is extraordinary the way things steamroll because if the young leave one farm, then the young on the next farm have less young to talk to, and so it snowballs. I am not saying now that money is not important but other things are important, as well. We can go through life saying if I had that much money I would be grand. A sister of mine, her husband died. And she said to me "Alice, money solves money problems. But there are other problems that money can't solve" and I thought: thank God. Because just at that time I thought there was nothing but money problems. We were up to our eyes in debt but I never forgot that.

FRANCES FITZGERALD

A Feminist from Army Barracks

Frances Fitzgerald was born in 1950 and educated at Sion Hill, Blackrock, Co Dublin, U.C.D., and the London School of Economics. She was Chairwoman of the Council for the Status of Women from 1988 to 1992 when she was elected to Dail Eireann, where she is currently the Fine Gael spokesperson on the Arts, Culture and the Gaeltacht. A regular contributor to social and women's journals, she is the co-author of Parenting - A Handbook for Parents.

My father was an army officer and I lived in Newbridge, Co. Kildare, until I was twelve. The Curragh barracks and army were part of the social scene, the class scene. Each group was a very clear entity; there was the army, and then the farming community, and the town community, and various other profess-ional groups. Growing up, I think that I was aware of my father's place within that structure.

At home we had all the basics but no excess. An army officer's salary was very low then, and my mother was at home full time. They managed on what they had, and got by. You did not feel that you were poor, but there was a striving for a standard. I was twelve when we moved to Dublin and my parents bought their own home. After that, they built a home and we moved back to Kildare. That was something they wanted to achieve. And they did so. There was certainly never any problem with basics like food and clothes, or tomorrow's dinner, or anything like that. But there was a contained feeling that money would have to be managed. However, there was always a nice feeling of security within that regime.

Lost Opportunities

My father was born in 1920. He represented that new generation of men who got opportunities through the development of the Irish State — in the army, teaching, the Civil Service, the ESB, Ireland as a state was coming into its own. When I was growing up he talked a lot about opportunity and justice, and especially the opportunities gained through education. Education was highly valued within the family, and I grew up with a strong awareness of equality and inequality, and the importance of opportunity. Opportunity is a word I use all the time now in relation to women. The importance of not putting people into rigid spots was something that I was aware of, and my father would also have been conscious of this because of the increased opportunities that there were for so many Irish people in the early years of the new state. Before that there was a lot of poverty, and things were slowly beginning to turn over a little bit and open up. That is what saddens me about to-day when I see the levels of unemployment. I feel that things have gone back for the vast portion of the population who are unemployed and haven't got opportunities. It is a strong contrast to the opportunities that were once offered by the state to earn a bit more money and have a good standard of living. In other words, to break into, the middle classes.

A Modest Sense of Success

My friends were all much the same, living in similar circumstances. There wasn't much excess around anywhere. That was my impression, anyway. I remember going to America when I was seventeen and thinking: God, I can't believe that children should have so much! My parents' aspirations for me were to have an education and to have a happy marriage. I think that agenda was pretty common then. That would have been their idea of success, to see me doing well educationally, and be happy and having a partner. It wouldn't have been the "you-can-do-anything" sort of success. It was more like next-step success. When I say that, maybe that is being a little harsh, because they would have been very encouraging: "you are as good as anybody else", but it wasn't terribly pushy, really.

Looking Back

I would have liked more of an open agenda. I would like to give my own children a very broad agenda;, I want them thinking that they can do anything. I think that is a really important message to give to children.

I have done therapeutic training, so I am very interested in this whole issue of the perplexities of family communication, and they are not easy to quantify or describe. I think the reality of most family life is incredibly complex and varied, and you don't really see the patterns until much later. Sometimes people never see them at all.

A general feeling about my own family: there was a lot of talking and emotions were reasonably open, but for all that there are so many emotions that did not get expressed. At the time I thought it was quite open, but as I get older and I look back, I can see that there were rigidities in certain areas. In the same way, I suppose, as other families in Ireland. But my impression was that my parents were open to me, and you could chat to them.

What Boys Do, What Girls Do

It amuses me when I think of the career options for my generation in comparison with to-day. We were hugely restricted and influenced by "what boys do" and "what girls do", and that would have influenced the subject choices. I went to a very good Dublin school when I was twelve. But my subject choices should have been much more interesting than they were, and yet here was I in a middle-class school in Dublin experiencing that. That leads to my wish now to see the whole area of subject choice tackled. Girls are not getting anything like the full choice they need to give themselves more choice in the long term, and better opportunities. I wouldn't say it was a family issue and I wasn't conscious of family restrictions as such, but it was the environment and the rules that existed at the time, and which are still there to a degree.

A Sense of Security

When I think of the strengths of my background the things that come to mind immediately are security, a sense of encouragement and comfort, of friendships, of being able to receive people, being sociable and linking with quite a range of people within the area where we lived, and a nice sense of excitement from time to time. It was predictable, if that is good. When I see families whose lives are so totally unpredictable and the problems that it causes, I can see how important a secure base can be.

We moved between a town and suburban Dublin. I became aware of a wider world although that was probably to do with getting older as well. I found Dublin much freer, but I don't think that was it really. I think it was more due to the fact that school had a much broader range of people. I probably became aware of a greater range of middle-class experience in that school, greater wealth, and a greater diversity of lifestyles. I hadn't seen that before, and then I saw it a lot, because it was South Dublin, a very established middle-class kind of area.

As I got older, it seemed that social order was more open. I think it was probably to do with the country becoming a bit more prosperous, more people going to university — that sort of thing. It just seemed totally natural that I went on to university. Fewer girls of my age and generation from the first school went on to college than the second school. I am very interested in the research on schools. All the research that has been done in

London schools show that the catchment of your school is a critical influence. I just thought Dublin more open after living in an Irish town, especially one with an army base. That was in the fifties and sixties. I don't know what they are like now.

Striving for a Goal

I think it is important to have a sense of striving for something and to a degree the middle class encourages that. If there is a fixed place surrounding you, it can blunt the striving. Also, I think it is good to have enough discomfort to kind of push you out the door and make you go for whatever it is you want. That has actually worked okay for me. But, when I see the lack of opportunities for many children of working-class families in Dublin at the moment, I certainly want to give people a choice of being a bit more comfortable with less need to strive.

One of my very early memories was back in primary school and being aware that there was a group of girls who came from poorer housing, who didn't dress as well. I remember the nuns giving them clothes and food. It is quite a strong memory. I remember feeling glad it wasn't me, but at the same time I questioned it; what is it about? What is the real story? It was difficult to understand, knowing that they were people who were exactly the same as myself, and good friends, but all the same there was a barrier. I had close friendships with one or two of the poorer girls, but not a huge number. I remember a kind of unspoken "something". I didn't known what it was at the time, but my parents would have said things like they are poor, or that they live in such a place. I had no sense of why they lived where they lived, yet I was aware that it was different. There was separation. That is the class separation. And it is still there. All the decision-makers in Ireland are men, and they are not just men — they are middle-class men. The girls' relations with me were mixed, now that I think of it. I don't know what words I would use; envy or jealousy might be a bit too strong. But I was aware of some sort of a flow, which I am convinced now, looking back, had to do with social conditioning. This is a sensitive area, because at a personal level these issues are very big and very real.

Barriers of Silence

One of the things the Council for the Status of Women is always trying to do is expose the silences that are there for women. There has been silence around battering; there has been silence around sexual abuse; there has been silence around so much of womens' lives or their work. It has been the same around class. Those silences are there, and they are in all of us. One of my earliest influences was being aware of that, and wondering why. How do you break down barriers? How do you communicate about them? It is a relatively unaddressed issue, I think.

My father had a strong model going back to his grandfather about opportunity and education; about the fact that people can get 'stuck' in society and that it is important to give people a chance to move forward. My uncle got a scholarship to teach in college. There were ways that you could progress. I would have seen that somehow it wasn't right. I think there should have been another message. If your family are in there and you are managing and striving well, then how much space is there to reach out and help other people? I would say I got those messages from my father, but there would probably have been another angle to it, namely an attitude of "get on with it". I went through primary school, secondary school, almost to university, without getting an explanation of 'the haves and have nots'.

How Society Works

I got to eighteen without any decent discussions around these issues. I was only beginning to get a grounding in the whole area doing Social Science. It wasn't until I went to university, that I really began to understand how our society functioned, how it worked.

I didn't really have any sense of "rich people". The only sense of that would have been probably the racing world, because of the trainers and so forth. And rich mightn't even be the word, it would just be a different world. My parents were quite interested in it. My mother knew Vincent O'Brien, as he was from the area she was from, so there was always great interest over Vincent O'Brien. He was seen as a model of success in this area for an Irishman. My parents got a great kick out of this.

My social-class situation now is much the same as when I was growing up. I have gone through university, I have continued as a professional social worker, I married somebody who is in a profession as well — a doctor. But my life is broader within the middle classes. I move in a much wider circle, but that is a sense of going up as well. It is a very wide field that I am involved in, in terms of class.

Vulnerability

The sense that you could lose everything, I am more conscious of that now. I think that is to do with an awareness around relationships around women, the vulnerability of women who are on their own. And another feature which has been unpredictable for many women; namely that in the future many women may become parents on their own, for example. It is those kind of things that I am much more aware of now than I would have been say in my early twenties. I have a much greater sense of the importance of independence for women.

Looking back at my own lifestyle. I see how relatively easy it has been from my early twenties, how privileged it has been. I think we say it is luck, but it is not luck. It is just about being born in a certain place and having certain opportunities. So many other things flow from that. To me that is the tragedy of it, that if you don't get those opportunities, so many things don't flow. I am amazed at how things logically do follow. If you move in a certain area, your partner tends to be from a certain grouping; if you go on the right steps of the educational ladder or the job ladder, there is broader vision and opportunities to participate in life, whether it is social, cultural, educational, economic or political. In a sense you take for granted your "middle classness" and the opportunities it gave you. If you are outside of that, it is so much more difficult.

Barred from the Bar

I remember discussing law at home, and it wasn't seen as some thing that was for me. That went back to the kind of restrictions of some middle-class thinking around opportunities. I was not conscious that, if I did certain things, they would lead to a certain place. It was more: you do your Leaving, go on to college, do social work, which was what I was interested in very much. But looking back now, I would have liked to have a sharper sense about career choice. If you do certain careers you are more likely to have opportunities, either internationally or within Europe. Or you will have more opportunities to contribute to public life. We are doing statistics on women now, and there are only two percent of women on the board of public companies. That is because women don't have a background in finance and accounts. If I had a daughter I would like her to arrive at eighteen with a sharper sense of direction about where things do and don't lead. I know that life isn't totally predictable, but I am just saying it is like helping children to understand society. I think the more awareness around these things the better, it opens up more avenues to people to develop their potential. So, what I am really talking about is a lifting of restrictions.

I remember the application I sent to UCD on social work. My motivation was interest and a curiosity in people and structures, and family factors, such as my father's own involvement in voluntary organisations. I had done surveys with him on people in County Kildare, going down to families in very isolated and poor areas. We were looking at people with polio at the time. I think those kind of things came together, plus what was on the table at the time. I was very motivated.

Understanding Society

I probably wished to understand society, and one of the things about my social work training which I am very grateful for is the sociological aspect and the sociological understanding of society and analysis; and I really did get a lot of value from that. I mean it wasn't a hugely developed analysis at that time; just what one gets in a primary degree. But I found it very rich and useful, I loved the whole sociology of education. Social work wasn't a choice to work with the poor. It was to work with people around service, empowerment, counselling and therapy. My analysis around poverty would come later. For me it was a way of working with people. That was more the model really. It wasn't around 'charity'; it was different.

When I was twenty-one my first job was working in a childrens' hospital (St. Ultan's) which has now closed down. I spent a lot of time up in Mount Pleasant Buildings, and all the issues then were around housing. There were dreadful housing conditions, children living in appalling poverty, and we would have them in the hospital for three or four months at a time because of the social conditions of their parents. I did an awful lot of work at community level, working with other community workers, trying to get things going on housing. I would be much more uncomfortable doing that now than I was then. I would have a different sense of awareness now. I see it as a much trickier kind of issue. I see social work more differently now than I did then. If I work with women it is empowering those women. Not to say that I wasn't trying to empower them before, but my understanding of it all is quite different now. It is about acknowledging difference a lot of the time and about trying to point out opportunities or helping groups to work out what they want to do for themselves.

It is not that earlier model at all: banging on a door of a housing department and push, push, push; though that has its advantages too. The whole way of social work is changing and moving towards statutory kind of control. It is a very uncomfortable relationship I think. I am not working in that kind of setting. I'm working more in a kind of therapy setting. Differences of social class, lifestyle, standard of living experienced in social work are so fundamental, but they are there in hospitals, in every service around the place you come to think about. What sort of impact do they have on different classes, client groups of professionals? We are all living it daily, but it brings out the challenges. Of course there is contrast in life style. What do you do about that? Do you stop working?

I find it happens within the women's groups as well. It has often been thrown around that this work is for middle-class women. I don't think it should be. I think this argument is often unfairly used against people. Social class differences shouldn't be a barrier; they shouldn't stop people who want to work for social justice.

I think that. But not all do so. There is work to be done in this area. As a middle-class person, experience is that you get a lot of stick when you start addressing the issues, those issues that are considered the preserve of certain groups. Your legitimacy is questioned; I don't think that should happen. I think that is both disempowering for the middle class and for the working class. How do you get the best out of people whatever the class? Where do you put class really? You don't deny the difference, but you don't let it stop development. The Council has made an absolute policy about flexibility. For example, there is no fee for affiliation, to encourage a wider range of women to get involved, and we have a very wide range of women's groups. But we still get this thrown at us by external groups: that we are middle class. My own sense is just to keep talking and discussing, and keep the dialogue going and try to work on the projects together. Just to get things moving. There are barriers there that, if they could be addressed a bit more, would disappear. Barriers disempower women. Now I know other people would feel differently; but all I can say is my belief around it is that, if some of these issues could be addressed, we would have a much richer kind of dialogue. We often take up an issue — say, women in decision making — and then we are often accused of only taking up 'elitist issues'. Like, say, getting more women into the Dail. I think if you have thirty or forty women in the Dail, you change the agenda for all women. Likewise if you could have women in all the decision-making areas I think the same thing might happen. I think decision-making is for women at all levels, not just for an elite group of women. It is about women in local communities.

Pathway to Dialogue

In acknowledging social-class differences, there is resistance on both sides, not just one side. It is always something that is very difficult for working-class women, but I think it is quite difficult for middle-class women also to find a pathway to dialogue. Both sides have difficulty, and that should be acknowledged. It is kind of a mutual problem, and a very interesting one to address. And it's the same with social work. Social workers should be much more radical now, with much more political focus on social action. It is a shame that we haven't really found a language or a way of working with social class yet. I think it is important that we do. We need to develop a way of understanding some of the complexities of action that are on every side. It seems that women's groups often want to just work away from men; women's groups work with women to deal with the kind of issues that come up. But a lot of that is around the class issue as well. Working-class groups working together and middle-class groups working together, working within their own grouping, and then breaking. I think very often what you have is a sort of premature attempt at linking, and then it goes wrong, and people retreat. I think you can say the same happens at a broader society level as well. I think there is a lot of work to be done on that, and I think generally in Ireland we probably haven't seriously addressed it. We haven't addressed it in relation to our politicians, for example. What is their experience with it, and how do they deal with it? And the whole constituency thing, and the local clinic — God, what is the local clinic? It is middle class, isn't it? The law, too; that whole interface is happening in our courts daily, and what is the experience really like for the two parties, what are the class issues that are hidden in there? And women's experiences before the law in Ireland — being a women in Ireland is one thing that alienates you in many ways from the law in this country. The law hasn't been very supportive of women in this country. And then secondly there is the class issue, so you have a double discrimination, in that area. So there is a lot of talking to be done around that.

A Single Issue

When you examine equal opportunities for women in Ireland, and the key issues facing women, they are not dissimilar, whether you are talking about working-class or middle-class, the basic thing is about income and dependency. For all women the issue is access to income. I think for many middle-class women who have access to some income, or who are maybe comfortable, it is because of their relationship with a partner.

But it is very unsatisfactory for a great number of women. Look at the whole issue of access to quality jobs. Employment is a key factor for women in all social classes. But of course, the direct experience of poverty makes it all the more critical to target women who have no experience of work, who have had poor education. So emphasis should be placed on return to work courses, return to education courses which target women who had no opportunities to date. I think the issue of women in decision-making affects all women, because if women feel they have more control over their local job centre, over their local community centre, over their local community facility or whatever it is, then that is empowering and leads on to other things. The health issues are critical, and I suppose middle-class women are a bit more protected in that area, but the incidence of health problems in working-class women is high, whether it is because of smoking or stress related. The statistics are extremely high around mental health, mental illnesses for Irish women, and these are depression-and class-related. Factors involved are: inferior conditions, relationships with partners, isolation, the number of children. In all of those, working-class women are more at risk than women of the middle class. So it is vital to build in protection around jobs, around training, around health, around better quality of service and education.

One could go on, it is a very wide agenda. The Commission on the Status of Women reported in 1992, and it is not accidental that it had the largest number of submissions ever made to a commission. Over 650 women from women's groups, who are from all over the country, and from all the social classes have written in. The enquiry crosses the class divide. Issues dealt with: taxation, social welfare, recognition of women, unpaid work; careers, whether it is unemployed families caring for people who are ill, or just generally. It is a very broad agenda for women in Ireland still, and it cuts right across class. There is a sort of positive action-targeting to ensure that women who are most needy get helped in a quicker way. I would target that huge group of women who are dependent on social welfare, who are in a poverty trap, the women who cannot live off social welfare. Even for the women who are motivated to get training and get a job, there is no financial incentive to move off social welfare. There is no child care to help them to make an easy transition from being dependent on the state, to becoming independent. And that is what many women want. I would start with incentives in that area, and child care would be a critical issue, because we still have a belief in Ireland that child care is a private responsibility. Since the economy doesn't need women in Ireland, there is no pushing to help women to move from the situation they are in.

Major Problem of Poverty

Given that we are talking about limited resources, I would target them in the direction I have mentioned; to begin to address the major problem of poverty among women found in Ireland, which is the critical issue for many women. That is really important. But I would also balance it with going for your quotas and your targets and everything else to get more women into the decision-making, so that you have a women's perspective in there and so you change the agenda. In Norway and Sweden and other countries, it has been shown that when you get more women in there, you change the agenda. You will get child care addressed, and issues which are of particular concern to women will get to the cabinet table, in a way that they are not now because you have mostly got men there. In national political terms, I think you have the critical issue of the democratic deficit regarding women's experience being reflected in decision-making, right through the system. Particularly at the top level. It has to be readdressed very quickly. If we wait for the natural order of events, before we even get to fifty-fifty representation that will be at least sixty years. It is too long. We can't wait that long, the generation doesn't want to wait that long, that's for sure. We will all be gone.

Minister for Women's Affairs

So you are talking about accelerated action, you're talking about willingness amongst men to share. It will affect men fundamentally, they will have to share within the family, outside the family and in the public arena. You will also have to have positive action-targetting to get more women into different sectors of employment, much more specific messages to young women about job opportunities and wider horizons for them, like they have done in England. British Rail and the Engineering Society send buses around the schools with information for young women on engineering, because it's a good option for women and there are going to be jobs in that area. Now that is just one small example. But you have to be really serious about this. The big problem, of course, is that in government there is no machinery turning the engine around, it is because there is no minister for women's affairs. That would be essential. Or else, if you have a minister for state, she really ought to have substantial powers to move the thing ahead, within all the different departments. Then you would see action. I mean the European Commission, the European Community, is excellent on all these areas. The recommendations and the language; it is all there for translating at national level. This goes back to the class issue really, that if Irish women could become a force together, all Irish women, — okay it is a grand view! — but really, if Irish women could work together, you could create a political will around these issues. While women are divided among themselves, it is a weakening factor, and that is why the issues we are talking about are critical. It would be a way of moving the thing forward, but it is going to take time. In the meantime we work away as best we can.

There are difficulties, and the class difference has to be acknowledged. But what I want to say is that the difference doesn't have to stop people working together. And it doesn't mean that at the interface people cannot be helped by contact with somebody, just because they are from a different social class, whether it is working-class or middle class. I suppose what I am saying is that, if we could have more debate about this class topic, work would be done more productively. The present interface is probably not the place for the debate, but the debate will help what happens at the interface. It would be a shame if the potential gets waylaid by what is really some unconscious class barriers or unconscious class messages that one or other party brings to that interface dynamic; I see that happen a lot, and it stops productive work, whether it is in the trade union movement (working with employers) or in the social partnership in government.

CARMENCITA HEDERMAN

The Virtue of Frugality

Carmencita Hederman was born in Dublin in 1939 and was educated in Sacred Heart Convents in Dublin and Surrey, before studying in Trinity College, Dublin and at the Sorbonne in Paris. An independent community alderman on Dublin City Council since 1974, she was elected Lord Mayor in 1987, and was a member of Seanad Eireann between 1989-1993. She is Vice-Chairman of the First National Building Society, a director of People in Need Trust and is on the board of Dublin City Food Bank. She is married to a surgeon and has five children.

Contrary to the popular conception, we were not well off. We lived in what today would be termed a big house. My father and mother had both come from comfortable backrounds. Nonetheless for a period we were not well off. I was born shortly after the out break of the war, a period of great stringency and rationing. And for both my mother and father, frugality was a virtue. It was a sort of Victorian trait. I only became aware of this when I married Billy. In his family it was even more noticeable and that made me realise that a lot of my parents' attitudes (which I thought had come from not being well off) were due to frugality. It was a virtue to be economical, to waste nothing, to conserve what one had and make the most of it. Even if people had money, it just wasn't considered right or proper to be wasteful.

I can't ever say that I went hungry, I suppose, yes, we were cold because we lived in a cold house, and we didn't have central heating, and we were exhorted to economise at all times with regard to the amount of heat or light that we used. We lived in a detached house surrounded by three acres in Stradbrook between

Blackrock and Deansgrange. We had two girls who helped in the house. At a later stage, we had three people which might today give an impression of being very well off but that wasn't the way things worked in those days. Help was a priority, and was inexpensive. My children find it very difficult to understand that in those days help was the last thing you could possibly do without. There were so few labour saving gadgets, there was a lot of hard work to be done and so you scrimped and scraped over things so that you could afford help.

It was the same thing in the garden. During the war my father ran a market garden. He had a quarter of an acre under glass where he grew tomatoes and all the family helped to pick, grade and deliver the tomatoes. He had a gardener and probably two men helping him, but there again that was quite normal in those circumstances.

Threadbare Uniforms

We went to school in the Sacred Heart Convent in Lower Leeson Street where there were four different uniforms. There was a summer one and a winter one, one for sports and a white one for special occasions. I didn't have a white one so I was kept at home on the Feast of Our Lady and on holy days. I was also very conscious that some of my uniforms were absolutely threadbare. There was a school down the lane — a national school — and I remember wishing that I attended that national school because there it wouldn't be so obvious if one had not got the uniform, or if it was threadbare, one would be just one of the crowd.

My husband and I have endeavoured to inculcate the same virtues of thrift into our children. Examples would be like turning off lights, not keeping the tap running when they were washing their teeth. We make certain the children turn off their heating before they go out to school in the morning, the penalty for not doing so is that they are not allowed to turn it on in the afternoon when they come in. It saves money and I don't see any reason why they should waste things. And the same would apply with regard to food. We never throw out a scrap of anything that could be used.

Family Life

Growing up we had very few pals. There were four of us in the family and our childhood was very family orientated. I am not sure if it was partly to do with the fact it was war time and travel was not very easy. The first outside contacts were with cousins, in particular a cousin of the same age who lived over in Clontarf. She is the first person I can remember having much contact with apart from my sister. We went to Brittas Bay for holidays, but there weren't many children there of my age.

I think I was happy. I am by nature happy with what I have and I didn't have much opportunity to compare myself with anybody else. We had plenty to do because we had a big garden in which to play. We were endlessly happy riding our bicycles around the garden and playing in the little stream or in our sand pit. We each had our own special patch of garden where we could grow anything we liked. We were quite resourceful as we made all our own entertainment. There was no TV. My world as a child didn't stretch outside the parameters of our house and our home, and within those I was perfectly happy.

Once a week only I went out and that was to go to mass on the back of my father's bicycle during the war. I did not go to school until I was about 6 years old because we had a governess who taught us at home.

Hindsight

Our parents had very lofty aspirations for us. My mother particularly. I suppose it is what every parent has for their children — that they should have the best, get the best. Her perceptions weren't by any means monetary or acquisitive. She would have set a very high value on our having the best possible education, and would have spared nothing to achieve this. It was essential for the enjoyment of a full and interesting life. I think, although my sister doesn't agree, that she was in her own way quite forward-looking. I don't want to say "feminist" because that word wouldn't have been part of her jargon, but I certainly didn't grow up with a feeling that because I was a girl I was any less able, or that I shouldn't have any aspirations that my brother had. My sister disagrees and says that my mother's aspirations were merely that we should be happily married to a nice well off husband and settle down and have a family.

It is terribly foolish to make judgements about people who lived in a past era by the standards of this era. If my mother had been born thirty or forty years later, I'm sure she would have held down a good job, had a full and interesting life and also brought up a family. Unfortunately in her day society didn't really permit her to do that, and I suppose it may have been frustrating for her, but I'm not sure she thought of it that way.

Conventions

One thing I found rather stifling about my youth was the over-emphasis on, the excessive concern about what other people might think, what other people might say. It seemed to dominate my mother's life and even as a child I found it very irritating. My father was the exact opposite and never cared a jot what anyone thought of him. On one occasion George, as we all called him, was going to the St. Patrick's pilgrimage to Lough Derg. When you arrive you have to hand in your shoes and go barefoot around the stations. My father, however, left his shoes at home and on the way to catch the pilgrimage train he called to his bank and marched into the manager's office barefooted and without any explanation. He was apparently oblivious of the stares. My brother, who was with him, was mortified.

Privilege

Though we may not have been very well-off I certainly grew up aware that in many ways we were very privileged but this brought heavy obligations. One of my mother's many sayings was "of those to whom much is given, much is expected." That was a basic rock on which our upbringing was based I didn't feel any sense of guilt or embarrassment that we were better off than other people, that we had better opportunities, that we had a whole range of advantages. That was just a fact of life. But as a result of that, more was expected of us. It put enormous moral obligations on us.

High Principles

My father was a very strong-minded person, very logical but rather too inclined to see things as either black or white. He had very high principles. I was very much aware of the fact that he was very sure of what his principles in life were.

The people in our world, apart from the family, were Hannah Dunne and Mary Gray, who were the cook and the housekeeper. There were also the men who worked in the garden.

Worthiness, Reputation

We were brought up to believe that we had a moral responsibility to give good example. Not only must you do the the right thing but you must be seen to be doing the right thing. People who had the advantages in life that we had bore a responsibility to behave honourably. My father spoke to us about a man's reputation, his good reputation; and he didn't mean it in just the sense of what people thought of him. He meant a reputation that was built up over the years. He was always telling us things like, it could take a man a lifetime to build up his reputation, and he could lose it in the blink of an eye by just doing something that was unworthy of him or which was dishonourable you know, or not the right thing.

My father's mother was a very forward-looking person and very strong willed. She was a feminist, if ever there was one. My grandmother was an extraordinary woman for her day, way ahead of her time, the first woman to drive a car and all that kind of thing. My father was a very clean thinker, very logical. I think he was a lawyer "manqué". And I remember growing up talking to him about things to do with philosophy or theology. I couldn't rattle him about anything. We were brought up when religion was, to a large extent, conventional. When I went to Trinity, I started thinking for myself and I was absolutely staggered to come home and to discover that there was nothing that my father wasn't able to deal with, or to cope with, on moral issues or social issues, or on anything. Now I am not saying that I always agreed with him. But he was always very confident, and he knew what he believed in, and he knew what his values were.

Respect for the Staff

We were expected to treat staff with the utmost respect. Not only with politeness, but consideration as well. I remember getting into terrible trouble with my sister when my parents thought that we were presuming on staff in any way, or behaving as people might be wont to behave. That was absolutely not tolerated, not tolerated at all, and my parents treated anybody working for them with the utmost consideration. I'm not sure it is the same today. Obviously things have changed and you know my children might say: oh God a girl working in the house had a terribly long day. She had to get up at seven in the morning, and she shared a room with the cook, those kind of things. But within the framework of the day I would say that my parents were the most considerate and thoughtful employers. My mother concerned herself with the well being of her staff. She would have concerned herself about their lives, or about what they were doing, and all that sort of thing.

I remember going to Italy when I was about eighteen. I went to teach a girl English. They were a big titled family from the south of Italy. They had a very similar family and set-up to what we had, I remember being rocked and shocked to the core of my being by the way the girl I taught spoke to and treated the manservant/butler that they had. They asked me to come and stay because the girl's parents were going away. And I said to the mother of the family I couldn't bring myself to come to stay if the girl was going to speak to the butler in the way that I had heard her.

I don't suppose we children thought that much about how staff might live or were very much aware of what their lives might be like. No, there was one exception. We had a woman who had been a nurse (a kind of a nanny) who had been in our house a good while. Then she had married, not terribly well. She had an unfortunate marriage, and she got fairly dragged down. My mother was very worried and upset and concerned because she felt that she could have done better for herself. My mother would have been worried that here was a girl who had the possibilities of a better life and she married a fellow who was an alcoholic or unemployed and, you know, not a great provider. My mother brought down clothes and helped them out in all sorts of ways. Now that exposed us to a different kind of world. She lived in a modest house in an estate in Blackrock and we often went there. However I wouldn't say that I ever saw an awful lot of depravation.

The staff treated me well. The only thing I can remember upsetting me was when Hannah, who was the housekeeper for years and years, told me over and over again that my parents wanted a boy instead of a girl and that upset me dreadfully. Other than that, I can't remember anything except happiness and security. My mother was a great homemaker and she wouldn't have wanted or she wouldn't have kept anybody in the house working or around her if they were not happy.

Haves and Have Nots

The message from school was that the world was divided into the "haves" and the "have nots" and that was the way that the Lord had ordained it. It was a fact of life. And we had to accept that and do our best for those who were the "have nots". We should do anything we could to make their lot a little bit less burdensome. Now what you really want to know is, did anyone suggest to me that perhaps we should help the "have nots" to become the "haves". No, not a lot of that I wouldn't think!

As I went to school, and got older, I quite definitely became aware of all these problems. You see it is terribly hard to know. All that I am telling you now is obviously me conditioned by my upbringing. But to what extent am I conditioned? If I had been born to someone different, would I have been as socially conscious? I am very patriotic and interested in people's welfare and so on, but how much of that was from my upbringing? And how much of it was the way I was born? It is hard to know.

Satisfaction

Definitely there were people in my life who were better off. I suppose there were certain things that you said, wouldn't it be nice to be like this or like that, but I think really I was very contented by and large. I don't think I felt a great sense of envy. Although we were aware of people who certainly were very well-off. Then you see my parents wouldn't have admired people just because they had money. I mean if you had money that was grand, but it had to be used for very specific things and definitely it wasn't for throwing around and making a show or for squandering, not at all.

I think I probably grew up imagining that the only people in the world who had a contribution to make were people who came from the same background as myself. I suppose that was the narrow-minded bit. Only from our generation (or from our background) came the people who ruled the world. That was something which I took quite a long time to overcome. It was only when I went into politics that I really started to appreciate the extraordinary contribution made by people from modest backgrounds who have never had any of the advantages or education that I have had. That is a source of great pleasure and satisfaction to me, to see people who have had very little and to see how well they can contribute in the very best sense, in all sorts of spheres. That was something that I was definitely slow about copping on to, because of the fact that our atmosphere was a bit rarefied. I can see my enemies reading this and saying "she is still rarefied", but I don't think so.

Inferiority

I grew up with a massive inferiority complex, in spite of everything that I have told you, but that was related specifically to my sister. We were brought up practically like twins. But she was two years older than me and my father's pet. He made no effort to conceal it. And everything that she did, everything she was good at, was considered worthwhile and the things that I was good at didn't get a look in. But nobody ever realises that other people have inferiority complexes, for with a lot of people it doesn't show. When I got married, and thanks to my husband who was always encouraging, telling me that I could cope, I got over that.

My mother certainly worked very hard to see that we went up the social ladder rather than down. It would have been less about earning well, less monetary, and more about class, if you know what I mean. We were never encouraged to marry a man for his money, absolutely not. Of course we joked, so-and-so would be a great catch. That would have been in jest. My mother believed that you marry your own class and your own creed, because she felt that was where we would make a happy marriage. She would have been upset if we had married foreigners but, having said that, both my parents were very outward-looking on Europe, but they considered we would have a much better chance of having a happy marriage (as they did) by marrying into our own class. My parents never used that expression, but that is what they meant.

A Good Marriage

Mind you, my parents' view of that would have infuriated us. We would marry whomever we wanted. I felt that it was terrible that these kind of things should restrict people in what they might do, or that conventions would hamstring or confine them. But I didn't exactly imagine that I was going to go off and marry a pauper either.

I don't want to give the impression in any way that my parents were narrow-minded or conservative. My mother was a bit of a contradiction. On the one hand she was bound up by the conventions, because they were there. Yet she had a marvellous ability to get the best out of people. She was also able to have a wonderful relationship with the cabinet maker or with the upholstery man or those kind of people who came, because she just got on very well with people. She greatly admired people who did their job well. It didn't matter what they did.

A Liberal Education

I believe that the value of a liberal education is in preparing people for life. My view would be that the poor, the less well-off, are those who most need these resources. Unemployment was unheard of in my day. I never knew of anybody who was unemployed. It was unthinkable. I say to my children "if you are going to be unemployed in the future, don't think badly of yourself for it. Unemployment is going to be a fact of life, but more importantly we as parents have to think how we are going to equip you to deal with being without a job." That is what I think is required of education. Not just points. I was three years out of school when I went to college, so I tell you that never gave me the idea that an education was in any way linked to earning my living, getting a job — that kind of thing.

I put store on the whole idea of people having opportunities and having education. It is a sense of wonder to me to see people who have to fight against the most incredible odds. They make it, and they manage to come out so successfully. I do realise that for me it was very cushy.

Class Consciousness

I wouldn't even be aware of different backgrounds. I am aware of it if somebody asked me a question about it, of course. But I find I am as happy and comfortable, and I enjoy meeting people from what I might call a deprived background, a very different background from mine. I don't think that I have any sort of guilty conscience about it because it is different from mine I find it stimulating to understand how they survived it, overcame it and coped with it and came out on top.

Where I Stand

There is a problem in identifying myself as left, right, or centre on social and economic issues. I would like to think of myself as to the left of centre but I really think it is very hard to answer that question because of the very dramatic changes and because the definitions are so totally different to what they would have been even a year or two ago.

I don't think I would be accused of being an extreme left-winger, but then on some issues, perhaps on some environmental issues, people would think that I was very left. On social issues I would hope that I am a liberal. If you wanted me to be specific I can say to you with regard to things like contraception, divorce, homosexuality, I am for liberalising the laws on all those but the only thing I am a hundred percent opposed to is abortion. Some people might throw me into the camp of the family planning and the family solidarity, to which I am absolutely opposed. I am clear about what I think about things. I am like my father, I like to think clearly what my view is on things and I don't wish to get involved in things, which is what really drives me mad about the Senate — people hopping up and talking about things that they know nothing about. I like to stick to issues, things that I am interested in and that I have the time and the ability (and to take the trouble) to go right down the road, about what I think about them. I can't do that with a hundred and fifty different issues.

MICK DOYLE

As Equal as the Next Man

Michael Gerard (Mick) Doyle was born in Co. Kerry in 1940. He was educated at Ranalough N.S., Dominican College, Newbridge, UCD Veterinary College and Cambridge University. Best known as a rugby player, he was capped twenty times for Ireland, and played for The British Lions. His first marriage was to Lynne Thompson from Somerset. They had three children, but later separated, although they remain in a business partnership. His new wife is Mandy Power Smith and they have one daughter. He is well known for his work in the media and for his autobiography, Doyler. A veterinary surgeon and companies director, he markets animal health care products which he has developed himself.

I was born in a beautiful stone house, built beside the first creamery my grandfather, Tom Dennehy, built in Currow, Co. Kerry, and lived there for the first twelve years of my life.

My grandparents were extremely well off. That was on my mother's side. And I had one grandparent on my father's side who was a merchant and fairly comfortable. My grandfather on my mother's side had developed a group of creameries, about five in all. It was a very prestigious business. He was the first man to export cheese out of Munster. The Kerry Creameries co-op bought them up in the '60's

Like Every Kid in the Parish

While they were well off and while they didn't lack anything, in that time (in the fifties and sixties) nobody was throwing luxuries around. It wasn't like what you would see on American

T.V. with kids being spoilt. I was treated like every other kid in the parish. I was probably in slightly better clothes, but I wasn't made to feel I was privileged in any way. I mean I was brought up normally without differentiation and I wouldn't have heard of the term 'class distinction' till a long time later. It would have been when I was seventeen years of age before I would have heard that terminology. It was a very happy world then but it was a harsh world in a sense. There was a lot of poverty, real poverty. People didn't have much and there was a huge disparity amongst kids going to school. But the teacher and the whole system of society tried to make things equal, as far as possible. It was a smashing period of time.

We had good food, good clothes, we had a fabulous house, in a big orchard, big lawns...everything was big. My folks were high achievers and highly intelligent. They were very normal people.

I was born in 1940. The war years made things a bit lean for everybody. There wasn't much wealth, real wealth, floating around. So there weren't many toys. But I got pistols and the usual things, guns and cowboy outfits, trains and the usual jazz. I started collecting Mecano sets at that time, that was a big thing I think, making your own gear. I had what I wanted, there wasn't anything that I needed, not really. Living in the countryside was a funny thing. I had dogs, cats and we used to chase rabbits and go fishing, I'd spend my time outside in the fields far more than I would playing with a particular toy. We were beside a beautiful old river and all the kids my age, boys and girls, were all playing around and mixing together.

Newbridge and UCD

My parents wanted me obviously to go to the boarding school where my dad had gone, Newbridge College, which I did. My mother had been to Drishane Convent which was near Cork, and then she had gone to finishing school in Monaco for a year or two. My parents' ambition for me would be to get a good education and be a well-rounded person and, if I were good enough, to go on to

University, to UCD, to get a degree and do something with myself. I think the old man's wish for me to get on the Irish Rugby team was nearly as strong as his wish for me to do something with myself. So yes, there was all that. It was gentle pressure. When I left Newbridge and went on to UCD, my first year in college was a hell of a heap, because I was thrown into the big city, from being in protective custody in a dreamy little college in County Kildare. Everything was disorientated and magnified incredibly. It took me a year to settle down and to decide exactly what I wanted to do, which was veterinary science. Dad kept writing about doing my work and studying, and I got pissed off. In the end I failed all my exams in the summer. Every damned one of them! I was doing a line with a girl who broke the thing off the week before we started our exams, which drove me spare because I had been going out with her a couple of years. I was only eighteen at this stage, and it was traumatic. I failed them all and had to go back in the summer to do a ten-week revision, and then sit the exam again. Two hundred and fifty others turned up for it. If I got it, fine, I was on my way into the Vet College. And if I didn't, I said to my old man: quit writing to me. I want to qualify more than you want me to qualify. And your writing to me won't do any good. It is just becoming monotonous. So just don't do it anymore, just leave me alone. I have my own ambitions now. After that there was no other problems.

Over-Pushing, Under-Pushing

The same happened me when I became a parent. You thread your way carefully between over-pushing and under-pushing. You have to pick some way where you stimulate the child to motivate himself, so you have to help him or her to show how to motivate themselves, rather than me motivating them all the time. I learned that at an early age. It was a big help. Then I was able to ask my father his opinion when I wanted it, which was far better for me and for him. So they were ambitious, but not overtly. They never pushed me in school. I had enough ambition from Kerry anyway, because it is a very competitive county. The education system is that way. Teachers cared. They still do. And it developed in me an incredible commitment to compete. I would compete at anything.

In Newbridge College they had a prize, a particular prize every year — apart from the prizes of winning at sports or for being top of your class. One prize I went after every year, which I won, was for general excellence in studies and games. I said, right. I wanted to be good at both. And I was. Luckily I was able to keep it up, because the same month I qualified as a veterinary surgeon, I also got my Irish cap and played in my first match against France. That proved to me that I could do it. It is a question of disciplining your mind and portioning out your time — proper time management and management of yourself.

Sure that was important to my parents and to me, they wanted me to be well balanced and they wanted me to achieve whatever I could achieve, whatever field I got involved in, to the best of my ability. Which was all they ever asked me to do, and that was fine. They weren't pushy at all.

Piano Lessons

My parents wanted me to play the piano and I hated it. They sent me down to a convent at home to learn the fucking thing, and I just couldn't make head or tail of it. It just drove me spare. I am musically minded, but... Dad was good at the piano and violin, but I thought it was a real sissy thing, so I never learnt it. I am sorry I didn't now. Maybe a lot of people are glad I didn't. I probably would be making a bigger nuisance of myself! I read an awful lot, I got that from my grandparents. My mother was very ill and my brother had arrived three-and-a-half years after me, so she had to look after him. I was put in my grandparents' house. I was under their influence more often than I was under my parents' influence, till I was twelve years of age or maybe a bit older. My grandmother had been a school teacher and was very intelligent, my grandfather was a business man who was well read and they had a library of books of all shapes and sizes from classics to whatever, so I had read most of them by the time I was twelve. I had been reading from a very early age, so that probably helped me to get a perspective on what I wanted to do.

I used to divide my time between Castleisland, where my parents lived, and Currow, where my grandparents lived. We had an uncle William who had a farm. We spent time with him and his kids making hay and those things, and generally fishing and whatever. We didn't need holidays. The first time we ever went away on a holiday I suppose I was eleven or twelve, we went to Butlins' and it seemed like a good idea.

Then we went to the UK. After that, we didn't bother much. We weren't big into holidays.

No Stifled Feelings

When I was brought up in my grandparents there were never any rows. It was a very peaceful upbringing, out in the country, and there were various uncles there who were going off getting married and doing various things. I think I got one clout in my life from my old man because I was missing for half a bloody day, with my young brother. They thought I had drowned him, or something. I was allowed to express sadness, joy, whatever way you wished. We had a lot of touching and cuddling and all that, so there was no problem with that. There was total relationship, which was easy. Both my parents and grandparents and uncles and aunts were all like that. They were very emotional. Ah they had God-awful rows and all that, but it was very emotional. There were no stifled feelings. You gave full reign to whatever you felt like at the time.

My family were mad letter writers. And we used to have debates and chats and everything. You learnt to get your point of view told or to fight for it from very early on.

Farm Life

On a farm you are very near nature. Things are being born and dying around you all the time. Something you miss in the city. Animals, for instance, their whole procreation, and the seasons changing. Your appreciation of why you are on earth hits you far more, your purpose, you are part of a design of what is there. I think you can come to terms with that. It gives balance to your life, it gives you the ability to see things in clear perspective, or it helps you to. It allows you to have a closer and more meaningful relationship with a lot more people that you trust. You learnt trust from early on, because you could trust people. While an outsider coming into our village would say, yes there is a big discrepancy in social standing here or social acquisitions and you know farms and this, that and the other. There may have been in an adult world but growing up we were totally unaware of it.

That is it, the strength of a rural upbringing is that it gives you confidence in yourself, gives you the ability to rationalise things for yourself and to make you feel that your values are important and that they are unshakeable and it does give you the ability to look it straight in the eye and say yeah that's it, that is my point of view thanks very much. And you have no fear of equivocating under that. You are who you are, and you know where you are coming from. That is what the countryside did for me. It gave me the ability to transcend an awful lot of contrived barriers or synthetic barriers or non-existing barriers, because it gave me the ability to communicate on equal terms with anybody. And to be at ease with anybody, no matter what level they were at. It teaches you that we are all the bloody same. Clothes don't make you, or money doesn't make you. There is an inner person to everybody, which you only see if you are in a society that doesn't distinguish, that doesn't penalise the distinction. I think that when it starts penalising the distinction is when it gets to the difficult stage. And when you get to the big city, the "have" and "have not" mentality can be explosive, as we see everyday in life.

There are no limitations to a rural upbringing. Not a single one. In the national school, the teaching I got was ahead of anything I ever had since. Without any question. The lessons I learnt, I still have. I was lucky I was born in the country, and I wouldn't wish to have been born anywhere else. I want to live in the country. When I am in the city I can take what I want out of it. In that way it is like wearing tinted glass. There was one thing that I found: that when I went to university, particularly the first year, naivety would have been my middle name. You get codded a couple of times and conned by guys who are much slicker than you are, but you learn dammed quick. I suppose at times you look at things in a more benign way than people that are worldlier and probably have been brought up in a more socially competitive stratum of society.

Culchie was a Fun Thing

Culchie was used as a fun thing, we had gone through all that in Newbridge College. The problem was that there were more culchies than townies, the Dublin lads were out-numbered by the Kerry lads and the Galway lads and the Cork fellows.

It was in fun, a kind of a relating term more than anything else. It was like being called a daft bugger.

Before the age of twelve you didn't have an incredible appreciation of social class. You wouldn't be measuring things in that way. I certainly can remember my grandmother taking me around a number of houses in the parish where some old people were living, and washing them and dressing them and looking after them, and making sure that the sons got off their arses and did something and grew spuds or some dammed thing. I remember small farmers, poor farmers whose kids had to milk the cows before they came to school. They would come to school crying, they would have had nothing to eat. They wouldn't have shoes in the middle of winter. That was then. It was quite incredible really. I had a fight every spring to be allowed to go to school without my shoes. I thought that was the best thing I could ever do, and I won in the end. I use to find everything wrong with my bloody shoes. You have this incredible need to be equal to everybody at every level. I don't know what it is. You don't want to be different. There was quite a lot of that kind of poverty. It wasn't measured in monetary terms. Houses were poor up until the late fifties. There was no electricity in our parish. We were the only house with electricity, because we had it from our creamery next door from the generator. The houses — going back and seeing them now, you wonder how in the name of Jesus did people live in those houses.

An Accident of Birth

We had lots of kids who would come and play at my house, and I would go and play with them and we would meet in school. Contrary to what you read about school today, there was no teasing of kids just because they were different. There was an understanding. The teachers were good, the whole system was worthwhile. It wasn't the achievers climbing up on everybody else and standing on them and consigning them to second-class citizenship. There was none of that. But it is very sad now, looking back on some of the people, what they were like and how they came out of it. They were smashing people. And brilliant. It was just an accident of birth.

My grandparents, worked hard and made money and they could buy things. That your parents were in business and could afford to get you a bike or to do something — sure you would have to love that. And you would realise how lucky you were. The overall feeling you would have would be of empathy and commiseration with poorer kids. That would stimulate you to give away everything you bloody-well had. I used to come home without half the things I went out with. I gave them away. You shared with kids, and I suppose that is human nature again.

The kids who felt they had nothing were probably feeling a bit bothered, a bit ashamed. But you wouldn't notice it at the time. The system in our school was quite unusual in that everything was shared around for a start. There were a couple of us put in charge of the bottles of milk, to warm them up at the turf fire. It was cold: you had no central heating in the school. Then you would share the food out. The teacher would ask the kids to show what they had in their school bags, so that the food got shared out. And if they didn't know their lessons, they weren't slapped. After school they were kept back for a half an hour to learn their lessons, so they learnt something everyday but they weren't intimidated or beaten up because they couldn't learn. They were coming out of homes where their parents weren't literate. They didn't have any encouragement to learn. There was abject poverty. They had to work their butts off before they came to school, and when they got back from school, so the only chance they had was in school. The parish priest made sure they got to school, and the absenteeism was very low. Sure, you would be aware, and sure you would try to do something about it. I suppose it develops a social awareness in you, and a social fairness.

I Leave My Car Outside

Workers around the house and the family business would be all friends of ours. I mean, I would know them well. The barber used to come cutting our hair, and fellows used to come in with the turf and wood. And there was the painter and gardener. I know them as well as I know my old man. They are all part of an extended relationship in an area, that still exists. I can leave my car outside with no problem. People know one another, and they help one another. I am sure that is the same all over Ireland. There is a community spirit.

There was no deferring to the boss's son. It's because of the relationship they had with my grandfather. When they had nothing, he built the creamery there, took their milk and paid them for it, gave them jobs, looked after them. It was from him it all came. If he had been no good, sure we would not have been singled out for respect.

I met guys in school, in Newbridge, who *appeared* to have everything. They probably hadn't, but they appeared to have — flash cars and so on. It was probably a lot on the surface, but they appeared to be fairly wealthy at the time. I didn't envy that, but in terms of coming up against real wealth I suppose Cambridge would have been a bit of an eye-opener. And Edinburgh was an eye-opener. People had an awful lot of money. People with wealth you wouldn't see in Ireland. You just didn't believe it could exist, because there was no real wealth in this country then. There is probably some now, but not in Ireland at that time. In Newbridge College we had about two hundred and fifty boarders and about fifty day boys, and we looked at the day boys as second-class citizens. That was so stupid really. When we were about fifteen or so we twigged that these guys were different because they weren't staying in the building. It would be stupid to be staying in the place when you live just across the damned street. Their clothes weren't as clean as ours, because we had laundry all the bloody time. And parcels from home. And we seemed to be better off than them. That was the first time really that I ever came up against any distinction, which was quite a daft one.

Decent Skins

When we met guys from other secondary schools, boarding schools like Glenstal Abbey, we thought they were a bit different. They had about five or six knives on the table when we had one, and they were probably upper-classish alright. We used to play them every year. Clongowes, we used to look down on them because they had crappy old buildings, whereas we had all fine new buildings. We used to reckon that Clongowes had the cream of the country — rich and thick. We were wrong of course!

I think everybody gagged up and just reckoned that Blackrock was just something else. You know, some guys went to school and other guys went to Blackrock. We thought they were good at rugby if nothing else. But you get these little prejudices. I am glad my son Andrew went there, though.

Disposable Readies

In U.C.D. social status and standing wasn't something that was cropping up. It wasn't a feature for most of us. I suppose because most of us who got to university were probably of a certain social standing anyway, our folks had to be able to afford the fees and digs and if they couldn't do that, there was no way you were ever going to get to university. Nowadays you can, with the points, grants and everything else. There wasn't an awareness of a discrepancy, but there was a certain awareness of disposable readies. I was on a set amount for five years, apart from digs money. I had about a pound a week pocket money, and thirty bob a week for lunches. That was that. The old man may have thrown in a few bob here and there, but that was what I was living on. I wasn't drinking, and we shared a lot of things. But I was never really aware of social disparities until probably after leaving university and growing up into a responsible adult. Probably in my twenties, my middle twenties, I became aware, that there was something.

Shoot the Planners

Poor people? In Dublin, Jesus you would want to be daft and blind not to see them. I mean there is total deprivation in some parts of the city. I remember the horror that we felt when Ballymun went up — bloody boxes stuck up, and them living out in the middle of nowhere. The saddest part of Tallaght was how the planners allowed some of those buildings to go up. It was really beyond me. I mean they should be taken and fucking well shot, because they showed no social or psychological awareness of anything. I mean plucking people up from the inner city and fucking them out in the wild. It is bad, bad, bad. I mean you destroy communities. You just make it impossible for people to evolve in an honourable way. Yes, there was a huge awareness then but the planners were psychological midgets.

I'm My Own Social Set

Class consciousness? I finally found it when I got on the Irish rugby team in sixty-four. When you are going to a party here or a party there and all of a sudden you become somebody whom everyone wants to talk to and wants to know. You see the whole bunch paraded around, in a social class in front of you, and you see the insidious march of social status, social standing, which is quite laughable. You see the scrambling to be invited, to be put on somebody's invitation list, and the ass-licking that goes with it. It is pathetic. It makes me laugh. It always has made me laugh. I have been fortunate in that I have never been stimulated to become part of a social set. I am my own social set wherever I am. I can talk to anybody. I can settle down on my own. I can go in and talk to a crowd of people, I can opt in or out as I see fit. Certainly not on the basis of money or acquisitions, real friendships yes.

Who believes that rugby per se automatically opens any doors you want? That is total crap. People want to be associated with achievement, no matter what sport they are in. The fact that an awful lot of rugby players, who are playing serious rugby, are middle-class people because they have gone to middle-class schools, that happens to be another accident. Rugby is played in those school as distinct from the Gaelic. It is not a parish game, like Gaelic football or hurling. It is not a city-localised game like soccer is. That happens to be the way it is. In the six counties of Ulster it is the national game of the well off. Soccer is the national game of the other part of the unionist populations. Gaelic football is predominantly ninty-nine per cent Catholic Irish Republican, whereas down here rugby is more of a non-class game, as Limerick rugby epitomizes so eloquently.

As Equal as Anybody

Social class to me is more to do with values and perception of mind and body and ability than any acquisitions. I always held that, and as long as I have what I have and am what I am, I am as socially equal as anybody.

Yes, sure, there were times I wished that I had taken the safe way out and gone for a steady salaried job which I could have done and been well paid for. But I prefer working for myself, and I prefer to make my own mistakes. I have made a few mistakes in business, I've been naive and been taken to the cleaners, and I've been on the brink a couple of times, particularly when I came back from New Zealand in eighty-seven after the World Cup when my business had virtually disappeared. I had to start from scratch years ago to get it built up again. But we have, thank God. There are a few good people along the way who helped us, both monetarily and with advice; but basically we did it ourselves. I have an in-built belief in me. Anything I want to do I feel I can do, and I go after it. I have learned to depend on people more. I have learnt to be a better team person. But I have to do the innovating, because only one person can dream. As long as you can dream and as long as you can work at it and find a medium to do it without being an island — because nobody is an island — and have the right people around you then you will succeed. The fact that I have done what I have done in different fields obviously has attracted the media and me. I have been in the media for such a long time now, and I have spoken my mind most times, and I'm pretty up front about things, I do things I believe in. That has probably enraged a lot of people, but it has probably satisfied an awful lot more. It put me on the same wavelength as a lot of people who know me from what I say, because they don't have to double think or double guess what I'm at. I think that is a waste of thought. Achievement is what you set yourself at, how you measure yourself. So as far as I am concerned, I have made as much use of what I have as I could have. But I would like to do a lot more.

I have done a number of innovative things in my profession in terms of disease prevention and animal health. Also part of my professional life is journalism now, which I like and which is very important to me. I like the challenge of it, I like the space I get, I like the openness about it. And it is good for me to communicate as well. That to me is my status, not a desire to have a bigger car or a bigger house. Whatever happens, happens. Fulfillment is more important to me, stretching for the limits of my ability.

An Irish Catholic Paddy

An interesting experience I had about defining one's social class happened in Cambridge University. In my first year there in sixty-five, at a dinner one evening where I was a guest speaker some bloke said to me, "I say Mike, do you mind being called Mick?", I said no that is my name. He said "over here Mick sort of conjures up an Irish Catholic Paddy" and I said "that is exactly what I fucking well am, an Irish Catholic Paddy thank you very much. Now have you any problem with that?" "No, no I haven't", "Well I haven't either. So call me Mick" The guy at least was asking me did I mind, would I like to be called Michael. Which I thought was touching.

I feel at home at any level of the social ladder. I believe in the dignity of human life, and I believe in the dignity of humans full stop. That is it. Irrespective of what bank they are with or how they are fixed or anything else. The fact that I have friends in a certain bracket is again an accident of the people I meet on a regular basis. So I have no problems or no hang-ups about it. I don't have any antagonism towards anybody for any reason.

152

Is Rugby Upper Class?

That rugby draws mainly from middle-class backgrounds I think is a huge loss. In Northern Ireland rugby is strong only on the Protestant side of the community. Catholic schools play Gaelic, or hurling. And there is a total divide between the two. In the south, in the Republic, you have the traditional boarding schools like Clongowes and Newbridge, the Castleknocks and the Blackrocks, Rockwells and Garballys who kept the game going for a hundred odd years. You have the big day schools like Blackrock, Belvedere, Terenure, Saint Mary's. You have Mountjoy, Columbus and Wesley — all those. You have Bandon Grammar, Sligo Grammar, Middleton Grammar, you have all those kinds of schools around the place. Then you have the clubs. You have senior clubs in the cities and you have the junior clubs in the cities and outside; you have a junior rugby club with the country clubs, town clubs and that kind of thing. But you also have a whole area out there that hasn't been tapped at all.

The GAA have a captive audience in national schools because there is a Gaelic football or hurling tradition out in the country. So the interest is in gaelic and hurling. And it is nurtured in kids up along the line. But there is an area where you have county footballers and county hurlers who just may be off the pace of their county team and who, if they had the right physique, would be naturals for rugby; but that has not been encouraged. We have to start at that level first, parallel to what has started in country clubs like Athy and Naas, North Kildare and Kilcullen and all over the country. You now have junior clubs starting off with kids' teams under nines, tens, elevens, and all that is starting. So it is gradually getting to the situation where a number of us are saying: it should have happened years ago. There was huge interest generated when Tommy Kiernan's team won The Triple Crown in eighty-two and mine won in eighty-five. But that hasn't been built on. I think Ireland's game against Australia in the World Cup stimulated an awful lot of get-up-and-go because kids saw excitement. There would be a perception that maybe the five nation championship — France, England, Ireland, Scotland and Wales — that has been going on for a hundred odd years, is a kind of elite club. But when the people see Italy, Romania (you can't call them upper class, right?) Japan (which have work teams from their car industry). and when you see the New Zealanders and Australians — somehow you know it isn't that kind of game at all really. It is a couple of assholes who have perpetuated that image of the chaps playing rugby, and that is it. It's wrong. As long as I have been on this side of the rugby line, other than total fools, I have never really seen any class bias whatsoever at the level I have been playing . I mean Limerick proves that. Kerry does as well. The junior clubs around the country have shown everybody that it is a myth. But again people like to have "I play rugby" on the C.V. However I think that's changing now.

Ruralizing Rugby

When it changes, when you get more and more of Irish country teams, the big expansion in rugby will not be up north. It has to be down south. And it will not come from the schools, because they are already producing as many as they can. It will come from the rural clubs, from the gaelic football tradition. Because it is an international game. The GAA was trying to mess around with this Australia rules game, and it won't work. It is not an international game. It is a *bastard* game and gaelic football is an Irish game and hurling is an Irish game and it will stay that way. People who aspire to represent the country, thirty-two counties of it, can see rugby as one of the ways of doing it, okay? As they are taught the skills of the game up along the line, their natural Gaelic football skills and hurling skills will be of enormous benefit to them. And that should be tapped. But whether this is going to happen, of course, is another question. When that emancipation of the game occurs, and it becomes spread across the whole country, then the Rugby hierarchy will have to change as well.

When you have had a dominant force of a certain section of the community who would be all professionals, they will now have to relinquish some position to the countryside to have a more democratic Irish Rugby Football Union. Then the trouble will start, and I can see that there could be a sense of "this could get out of hand". We could have a real national team here, or a real national game. And I always have the sneaking feeling that people are afraid to lose their positions of elitism as administrators of an international game. Even though they have done a good job, it could be under threat.

More Paddys on the Team

I think Rugby just has to become more broadly based. It will make the game a far more supportable game. To an awful lot of people it will popularise it to an incredible extent, and it will give it more support. It will bring players, more players, into the game and cut out the stereotyping that is knocking around. It will bring more talent into the game, and it will probably bring more democracy into it, into the administration too which has come stereotyped as well. I admire the Irish Rugby Football Union as a body of people who administer the game and who have the ethos of the game in mind. Compared with the GAA, I think they are light years ahead. They are far more switched on to what the game is about, where it stands in Irish life and what its opinion is and what it wants to do. I think it administers a very good game and it is a very financially well-run organisation. It probably doesn't move as quickly as a lot of us would like it to move, but the administrators are probably right. As for ruralizing the game, I think they have to do that much quicker. We need more strong country players, with strong bloody arms and arses on them and not some of these cream puffs that are all blown up with weight training. I don't want to see that. I don't want to see purely gym-built players on the Irish team. I want to see more Paddys on it, and the sooner the better.

JOSEPH O'CONNOR

Desperados Waiting for the Tube

Joseph O'Connor was born in Dublin in 1963 and educated at UCD. He is the author of two novels, Cowboys and Indians and Desperadoes and a collection of short stories, True Believers. A brother of the singer, Sinead O'Connor, he now lives in London, from where he writes a column for The Sunday Tribune. He has received many literary awards.

Discussions of class are very fraught anyway, it depends exactly how we define these things. My mother's family would have been working class, but originally from a rural background. Her father was a breadman. My father's family were a kind of strange sub-section of working class. His father was a carpenter, a cabinet-maker. They were from the Liberties area of Dublin for several generations, where my father's grandparents had owned a small shop. So, in a way, I suppose you would classify them as working class, although they were actually petit bourgeois if you like. Or working class people with middle class aspirations. So that it is that kind of mix. But both of my parents certainly knew poverty in their childhoods.

Becoming Middle Class

I think my parents changed class if you like, I think they were typical of many people in Ireland in the late fifties and sixties who were working class but who aspired to being middle class. I think they *became* middle class. It is an interesting thing from this generation's point of view because we are really the first pure middle class generation. You know, your parents still have the working class standard in the background, but you are the first solidly middle class one. It is not like the British class system where the middle class has existed for a lot longer. It is slightly disorientating but anyway that is just to sum up working class people who became middle class and very deliberately set out to do so.

I would say my upbringing was in a middle class family. It was a very typical Dublin middle class standard of living; I mean mainly private education which is one of the ways in which I would actually classify classes. I think if you pay for your education that means you are middle class. I had a very nice house and, you know, trees along the roads, holidays every year.

Typically of that generation of middle class people, my parents weren't privileged, it wasn't a question of inherited wealth. These people became middle class through their own efforts based on my father's work as a self employed engineer.

Our standard of living was fairly constant, I mean there were peaks and valleys but it was reasonably constant. I think we were brought up with that certain sense of security, you knew the day was not going to arrive when the bailiffs would come and take the furniture away. It was generally very good, very comfortable.

Looking back now I think I would have been as satisfied as most children. Funny, I can never remember wanting one particular material thing and not having it. As I say it was a very privileged middle class upbringing.

We had about the same as other children, because like most middle class children you only know other middle class children. You know the children who live on the same road, and you know the children you go to school with, all of whom in my case came from very similar backgrounds. So you had a certain sense of a cosy life or world. I should say that the working class strand in my background, in my parents' background was always very strong. I think my parents were always very proud of their background and not snobbish at all. They detested snobbery and were very proud of where they had come from and tried to convey a sense of that. I think we were slightly different to children whom we would have known and who we would have been in school with and whose parents would desperately foster the middle class thing and wave the middle class flag as long as they could.

Owning the Merc

People would have perceived my family as fucked up. My parents were decent people who loved each other, but they weren't lucky. I think it is probably not relevant, but I mean I came from a very unhappy family background. Economically we would have been seen as a very well to do family and my father, curiously enough although he is not very flash, always had to have very nice cars. I think that was the one kind of indulgence, the Mercedes car; the big thing was to have the car, you know? I think we would have been seen as very comfortable and something the whole world should aspire to.

I think because both my parent had to struggle very hard for their own education, and it affected them and us in a kind of curious way, which was slightly different to other peoples' parents. We never had any pressure to become professionals, you know, accountants or solicitors or lawyers. It was very much a case of education for its own sake while we were in school. I had no pressure at all careerwise, just to do the best you could and try and enjoy the education and try and enjoy the world of books and learning and culture. And whatever happened after that was fine with them. So they didn't put any pressure on us to perform to the middle class norm, which I am very grateful for, because it does crush people's ability and individuality. Perhaps because they were unhappy themselves, that may have something to do with it. I think it altered their priorities and it altered ours so maybe we weren't pushed into those things. I don't think they had any aspirations for me as regards academic achievement or careers.

Success in their terms was very personal, not to measure up to the public recognition of money or having a big house, very much a personal internal thing. Just being at ease with yourself and the world and doing whatever you could to make the world a better place; those kind of notions which formed their ideas of what success was.

Unhappiness a Good Thing

Their thinking came from two sources. Firstly, I think there is a certain strand in Irish or in Dublin working class culture, the sort of self educated thing, which both my parent were. My father left school when he was thirteen but had a fantastic love of books, poetry and drama. My mother too. I think because it had been hard for them to have access to that kind of worlds, they wanted to make it easy for us to have access to it. Part of that was keeping the pressure off in terms of what we would be doing for a living and just opening the doors to these other kind of worlds. Secondly, I think a degree of unhappiness is probably quite a good thing because it does alter people's perceptions and their desires and it means that, you know, maybe the most important thing in the world isn't a nine to five job with a pension at the end.

I think my parents approval was not demanded as much as it was in other families. There was a degree of freedom to do what we wanted to do and there were many times when they neither approved or disapproved, just kind of maintained a benign eye and on what we were doing.

Hardly the Waltons

Feelings *were* expressed in my family. I mean particularly anger, particularly the nasty end of the spectrum. But I think the other end of things too, I mean my parents were very open usually. I don't think any of us have any hangups about expressing affection or emotions.

Expression of feelings was permitted yes, but I wouldn't say encouraged; I wouldn't say they were actually gushing about it you know. We weren't the sort of kids that were tucked up in bed every night and they didn't tell us that they loved us every single night of the week. It certainly wasn't The Waltons but it was very open, for people of that generation for whom all that was a very difficult thing. Again I think we were lucky that our parents managed to get that together some way.

I wouldn't describe my parents as being composed. They were both very passionate actually but I don't know if that is a class thing, or a kind of individual psychology.

As for the strengths of a middle class background there are a few and I think they are mainly economic. I mean I think the benefits of being middle class are that you don't have to worry about poverty.

I think it is definitely beneficial to people's emotional well being, their creativity and political sense as well. I mean, if you are poor the chance is that you are not going to be interested in changing the world because you are too busy just surviving. Middle class people can afford the luxury of thinking, wouldn't it be good if things were a bit better. As a result I think a lot of left wing politicians come from very solidly middle class backgrounds. I think it frees up that area of people's political creativity.

A middle class background has its downside too, a kind of detestable, materialistic, complacent, cosy, "I am alright" way of looking at the world. Life is just about *having,* and protecting yourself and possibly the family, the family unit. The middle class institution I think should be completely destroyed. The cosiness I hate, it just irritates me.

Them and Us

Middle classness involves a lack of compassion, a worry about dividing up the world into us and them. And us is a very small number. "US" is you and your family and a very small number of people against "THEM", you know, the rabble out there. You have it hard thinking that you will ever become part of this rabble again or that your children would ever become part of it. Every thing is geared towards their "education" and their "career," on launching them on exactly the same empty little cruise through life that you had yourself. Those kind of attitudes are really detestable for me. I think that is the downside. Thankfully we didn't have that in my family.

Contact with Other Social Classes in Childhood.

Yes I mean, I think I always knew Glenageary where I lived was not the world and that there were other world's where people were not as privileged, you know half a mile down the road. I think I was aware of them, I would describe a lot of my parent's siblings as still being working class. I suppose my cousins would have been among the few working class people of our own age that we would have met. I think we were aware that my grandparents, — both sets of them — were working class. So yes, we were aware of where we had come from.

Outside the family we would have known they were there but we didn't have personal contact with working class people. But I never thought that we were that different ourselves. It is probably very boring to keep going back to this — but because we knew where our parents had come from and we had access to working class values through them, I think I never saw myself as completely different and so would not have fantasised about the wonderful world of working class attitude. It is a curious thing. Accents, as well; because if you grow up in an environment where everybody has a middle class accent, well, I think language re-enforces class very strongly. Both of my parents spoke like real Dublin people so I think this would have shored up the notion that we weren't that different from working class people. They were kind of working class people with money.

I mean my parents detested snobbery, they didn't encourage us to think we were better than anyone else; so there was no us and them and hence there was no artificial curiosity about what "them" might have been like. Any information my parents gave me about working class people, not particularly gushing or anything, I mean it wasn't the heroic proletariat. But I think it would have been informative without being value-laden.

Coded Messages of School

On the other hand school gave me very coded messages about the working class and, you know, they fitted into, I suppose, the general Catholic view of these things. The Lord may have made all things bright and beautiful but He also made the rich man in his castle and the poor man at the gate. I think the image of poor people would have expressed itself in this way. I explained to you that we would be invited to bring in tins of whatever we could find in our mothers' kitchens at Christmas and Easter and there would be a collection for the poor or as they were referred to — "the people who were less fortunate than ourselves". It is a phrase that resonates still in the back of my mind. Even at that age it struck me as a curious notion that people are poor because they are less fortunate than other people. In fact people are poorer because of political systems which *make* them poor and which thrive because some people *have* to be poor. It was just a little shorthand version of the way the church coyly de-politicises the issues and turns them into games of chance rather than issues of politics that we can actually change. I suppose that kind of notion — the poor were to be pitied and all that but given nothing much more than a tin of pineapple chunks at Christmas.

I have memories of individuals, there was always you know this spoiled brat who had a nicer bike than you and families who went to Disney Land and all that stuff, I wouldn't have seen them as a class. I don't know if there is an upper class actually in Ireland but if there is I certainly wasn't aware of it then.

Contact with Other Social Classes

I try my utmost not to evaluate people I might be spending time with on that basis, so there is no class that I feel more comfortable with than any other. I suppose in the way of these things most of the people I know are middle class but I would like to think of that as a coincidence. That is probably a complete rationalisation. But I don't evaluate people in that way.

I have close friendships with some working class people. I think discussions like this would probably get in the way of a friendship with a working class person. Being very self conscious about one's class or very hung up or guilty about it, those kind of things would probably get in the way. I am not particularly guilty, I am sorry to say. I am not hung up about it and I don't evaluate people on that basis. But probably my contacts are about eighty percent middle class.

I think what is important about privilege is to use it to change things. But guilt is a very destructive emotion and leads to a patronising political view of the world. So I wouldn't waste my time feeling guilty about the lot that fate has dealt. It is much more important to channel your energy into doing something to change things.

I think our society sets a sort of quite narrow limit on humanity but it doesn't dehumanise the middle classes. I mean it is a very middle class society, middle class is what you aspire to be in Ireland, the peasants taking over the castle, everyone wants to be middle class so it is not dehumanising. It is supposed to be what we all want. It is not very enriching.

It is very narrow, *our* view of the world, very conservative, *our* theology, right wing touches with a bit of liberalism, you know, be nice to the blacks because we don't have any living on our road. That narrowness I suppose.

164

A Strange Purgatory

I wouldn't consider myself to be middle class these days, to be honest. I think writers are in a sort of strange purgatory, I suppose, when it comes to discussions about class. Because at one level you are self employed and at another you are a crazed creative loon in the attic. It is a slightly schizophrenic existence in which received notions of class don't actually help very much. So I am classless really. At least that is how I think of myself. But middle-class people are very good at claiming to be classless. Perhaps that is the most middle class thing I've said in the entire interview. I think it probably is.

I suppose the political direction that makes sense for middle class people is the sort of direction that we have had since the foundation of the state. If you were to look at it scientifically that *must* be the direction that makes sense for them, because that is what we have always had.

I have been interested and active in left wing politics since I was about eighteen and that is very important to me. It is a big part of my life and all that. It sounds very moralistic but I think privileged people *should* do it. I think it is a moral imperative to work to change the system and get rid of these miserable notions of ours and try and make things more equal and share things out more and more democraticly, pluralisticly. Those ideas. They are important.

A lot of my interest in politics is very personally motivated, it is not particularly about helping others you know. *I* would like to live in a fairer world. It would make *me* feel good, it would make *me* feel, you know, life is a bit more worth living. But I mean it is a selfish thing. I try to avoid that do-gooder stuff, I can see where that contradiction would have expressed itself but all politics is dialectical. That is how history, how change happened. So even if that contradiction was true for a lot of people I wouldn't worry about it. I mean the French Revolution happened largely because of the middle class but it is a good thing that it happened.

165

I've got no money, if that is what you are asking me. I suppose I probably still am riddled with middle class aspirations in one sense. I mean I would like to have somewhere nice to live and I would like to not have to worry about the phone getting cut off, I would like to go on a holiday once a year. I don't have all of those things just at the moment. So I suppose economically it is not a plummet but it is a gentle slide.

But I think the future path is actually a huge chateau in the South of France where I can go and live in great richness and worry about the working class of the world, and when are they going to start the revolution.

Inheriting the Farm

In Irish terms, I mean the Irish literary tradition was an ascendancy, after Independence it became a literature of a kind of urban working class and small town rural Ireland. And that is really what we have had all the way up to now. There aren't very many people who can write about the middle class and the suburban in Ireland. It is all about being Catholic and living on the edge of a bog and waiting for someone to die so you can inherit the farm and all of that stuff which has been done, you know, brilliantly, but by other people. So I guess I am kind of lucky in a way. The world I feel attracted to writing about is the world that I happen to know very well. I think it is important that somebody chronicles what is going on in middle class Ireland. It is not something that I would particularly like to be doing for the rest of my life, myself. But it is important that somebody does it.

I've been criticised as a writer for being middle class. It is like somebody criticising me for the size shoe I take. So I don't engage in that side of things at all and anyway I have reviewed books for downmarket newspapers myself from time to time, so I know precisely how little thought and effort goes into doing it. So that doesn't worry me too much, you know, that is fine.

There is an ideology that constantly pushes at, you know, we have to have gritty urban novels about kids shooting up on heroin and drinking cider on the railway tracks or else we have the rural stuff. People like all that, that is what they are used to and it is very hard to interest people in anything else so I suppose that is the reason for the criticism.

A Growing Class

Demographically the middle class is growing. Although that is true, I don't think that is reason enough to write about that world, I mean you don't write on that account. You write because stories and myths and chronicles of peoples' desires and fears are important. They say something to us about our own lives and my hope is to make sense of them. I think all fiction deals with very similar themes. We all get bored, we all grow up and we all have relationships with our parents, and we fall in love and fall out of love and back in love again and have children and we succeed or fail and we die. There aren't that many stories, you know? They are about ordinary peoples' struggle to understand their world and I think just because those characters happen to be middle class, doesn't mean that those struggles are *necessarily* less important or less sophisticated struggles than those of working class characters. It is another world to write about but it is the same old story.

I think with my stuff people who might get lost are probably people who are most lucky in terms of background. I think what you are trying to do is always define the universal in the particular. So an instance in my book, a scene between a father and son and an embarrassed avowal of affection between them, of course it is just meant to be about those two people but it is also meant to be about any father and son. It is supposed to be about all fathers and all sons. It can probably fail but that is what it is supposed to do, that is what it is all about, finding the world in the lives of your characters. You know it is important to try to do that.

I wasn't brought up in a tenament in nineteen-twenties Dublin but I think that Sean O' Casey is great and I have never been to Denmark but I think that Hamlet is great. I think that is the way people work, people have a need for stories, people like mythologies. They inform their lives and it doesn't matter if the mythology in the book is not in every single detail the mythology within which you live your own life. It just informs it and colours it and maybe it even contradicts it and makes you hate it. But fiction makes people think and it makes them feel and it is those aspects of it that are interesting, not the chronicling of middle class life just for the sake of it.

I had the best education the taxpayer could buy, you know. Mainly, the taxpayer in my own family. But I mean that was a help to me. To other writers, that may not be important. But in my case being allowed to go to UCD and read wonderful novels for a couple of years was a great help.

LORD INCHIQUIN

Irish Chief, English Accent

Born in 1943, Conor O'Brien is The O'Brien of Thomond and Lord Inchiquin (18th Baron). He become Chief and Peer on the death of his uncle in 1982, and lives in a modern Georgian house on the family estates, next to Dromoland Castle which was turned into a luxury hotel by Bernard McDonough in 1963. He was educated in England, served in the British army and worked for most of his life abroad, finally in Financial Services in Hong Kong before returning to live in Ireland, where he married Helen Farrell of Longford. They run an exclusive guest house at Dromoland. He believes that The Irish Chiefs can play a major role in the cultural heritage of Irish life.

Family of Origin

I think my family would be termed upper-class. It is difficult to break it down further than that, apart from the fact that it might be termed aristocratic upper-class or old upper-class, as opposed to newer upper-class.

Old Family Retainer

Just because one terms oneself (or other people term you) upper-class doesn't necessarily mean that you were born either with a silver spoon in your mouth, or with a large house, or with fine surroundings. I was born in England during the war and my father was in the Royal Air Force, as were his brothers and sisters. I lived (was born, in fact) in my grandmother's house, which was a reasonable sized house in Surrey with one servant, Michael, an old family retainer. He had been with my grandmother for years as a cook. We did have a staff then; of one. The war years were difficult and after the war we moved to Camberly and then Dorking, and we lived in small houses, nothing ostentacious. We didn't have any money. My father wasn't making very much money, he didn't inherit any, being the younger son. In other words his elder brother, who was then Lord Inchiquin, inherited the land and estates and most of the money.

So from that point of view I had a normal upbringing, I went to school in Dorking, to a small primary school, and then at the age of eight I went to what is called a prep school to get ready for public school. A fairly sparse upbringing there, you were rarely allowed out in the town. Not like now, where if you are in a boarding school you come out every weekend. So a traditional English upbringing, prep school, public school. I didn't go to university, but I joined the army and went on into life.

Days of Rationing

No, money didn't come father's way. They were difficult times. Rationing was still going on in 1955, so there was still a lack of food. But it was a good family environment, a good home. We weren't sort of on the bread line or anything like that; but we didn't have all the comforts. We didn't have a big car, we didn't have staff, we didn't have any of those things. So you might say that I was sort of brought up normally.

For the summer holidays we went down to the coast, to the sea. We went to Cornwall a few years. We never went abroad, I didn't go abroad until I was sixteen or seventeen, when I went to France.

Prep School

I went to a prep school called Fancourt, which is a boys' boarding school in Surrey, and then I went to Eton College which is traditionally a family school. My uncles and grandfather had been there. It was very much a traditional upper-class type of education.

In the public school you had a complete mixture. You had extremely wealthy, you had titled people, you had poor people. You had old money, new money, a complete mixture.

I tend to remember the better times and try to forget the worst. But overall I enjoyed it. There was very strict discipline. I was beaten two nights running for what they call mobbing, beaten with a cane. Old traditions which would have now died out but didn't do me any harm. You had to work hard, you were taught independence, you had to pass the exams at the end of each term, which was called a half. If you failed those twice, you were thrown out of the school. Homework was done entirely on your own, there was no supervision. If you didn't get down yourself and do your homework, even though it is a public school, then you would fail your exams. You were taught from an early age a degree of discipline and independence so that you would get on by yourself and do things.

A Tolerant Bunch

I had pocket money, something like one and three pence a day, which was reasonable. Some boys had lots of money; you would have some friends who would have more money than you, and they tended to buy things and share things with you. There was never a sort of jealousy over money. Some boys flaunted their wealth, that tended to be the new money or the nouveau riche as it is sometimes called. Then of course on parents' day you would see a lot of Rolls Royces, Jaguars right down to the old Morris Minor. I think that is part of the reason why I would say basically upper-class people are a tolerant bunch because they had exposure to both the wealthy and the poor in their own system, and learned to adjust to it. It is a relative poverty, obviously, compared to poverty in the working class. It is something that you learn when you are fairly young. From a class point of view most of the boys in public school are considered upper-class. Or were. I am not so sure if they are now.

The Slums of Limerston Street

I think a lot of people tend to think of the upper-class and aristocracy as a bit of a dying race, that a lot of them are impoverished. From day one in your upbringing, you are brought up with boys or children from similar type families, in other words boys you go to school with at prep school are from middle- or upper-class families. You are not at that stage mixing with or playing with working-class children. Mind you, when I moved to London in 1951, we lived in a street called Limerston Street which is in Chelsea. The slums were just being cleared, the houses were being redecorated in Limerston street. We were about the fourth or fifth house which had been done up, so all around us was still slums. I used to go out and play in the streets with the kids and it didn't really matter. They may have at times poked fun at you and maybe we had more pocket money than they had.

A Gentleman Not a Yobbo

My parents wanted me to go through the educational system successfully. They weren't looking for a genius or anything like that. They were obviously wanting me to go through the schooling system, either to go to university or to get into some trade or business after school and to turn out a young gentleman, as opposed to a yobbo. Obviously my parents wanted me to be the same as they were, but that is true of every generation. When I was growing up in the fifties, the time of the teddy boys, I didn't become a teddy boy, but I used to wear drain-pipe jeans and I am sure my parents didn't think much of that. Nowadays it is earrings or long hair. So each generation is different. But their aspiration was that I would turn out okay and get on in life. I don't think they wanted much more than that. I didn't work hard at school, I didn't do well enough to go to university. Not that they particularly wanted me to go to university. But I passed okay, reasonably okay.

My parents weren't forcing me. Basically they would have been happy for me to go into anything that I wanted to do. Probably they were disappointed that I didn't do better at school and have the opportunity to go to university. Now having been through my life I am quite sure that they think what I did do was fine. Again I continued on a traditional theme of the upper-class: joined the army, joined the foreign office, joined the merchant bank. Any of those sort of things were acceptable occupations, and I chose the army. So from their point of view I turned out okay.

Expression of feelings was reserved. And I think that is one of the results of the upper-class type education. You are sent away to at an early age to boarding school to learn the tradition. Also you tended to have fairly strict discipline as a child. I had a nanny for the first year or two years of my life and my sister's life, and then after that we had "au pair" girls and we were disciplined. We were in bed by six and we didn't have television or anything, so we lived a fairly disciplined, hard life. This tends to draw you away from the very close family system. That doesn't mean to say that I am not close to my family; but in a different way. That shows in the way that one expresses oneself.

Stiff Upper Lip

I think again it is the upper-class system which perhaps does that, but that doesn't necessarily mean that everyone is like that. But in general I would say that type of upbringing and education tends to repress feelings. I mean if you are mad or whatever you can shout and scream but you probably wouldn't swear, although I have sworn in my life. But whereas different classes express themselves in different ways either by hitting someone or swearing at them, we tended to have a higher tolerance level. We very seldom hit anyone. We tended to use words more to get ourself out of trouble. I have only once ever had a sort of street fight situation. You tended to use your brain more to get out of those sort of situations.

I have a sister two years older than me. I suppose girls are closer to their parents. Maybe they have not quite so strict an upbringing, so maybe they are more expressive.

The best parts, if you like, of the upper-class upbringing is discipline, tolerance, being able to get on with people, being able to motivate oneself, teamship, working together as a team. There is a high emphasis on sports in school, particularly in England, and I think we should change the emphasis more onto sports in Ireland. I think that sports are one thing which brings everyone together. It doesn't matter who they are, they are all wearing the same clothes.

Learning About the World

I could be viewed as having had a narrow upbringing. You don't get streetwise, you are living in an environment that protects you from the outside to a certain extent and when you leave school, you go out into the world, maybe it is more difficult to acclimatise than as if you had been brought up in a different way. But then I think the attributes you have and you have learnt in life, in your school days enable you to get on, because you are tolerant. You become worldwise in a different way.

I don't think boarding school at a young age is cruel for boys. For girls yes, but things have changed now. The school systems have changed and it is not so much like a prison. If you have the choice of education (which I think one has to have) it is a good system where you have both state schools and private schools. Those who want to go to private schools should be allowed to go. I mean they pay for them. It is a privilege. It is a choice. And I don't think a state should be allowed to dictate an educational system to everyone. To send a boy of eight to a boarding school is fine, because that is where he is going to learn, that is where he is going to make friends. He is going to learn comradeship, he is going to play sports which I think he needs to have. I think all

children should play sports compulsorily every day. Every afternoon they should be out in the fresh air.

The Children Out of One's Hair

Boarding school takes you away from your family environment
for long periods, so you lose a certain amount of a closeness to
the family environment. Many parents, particularly if they have
got difficult children, would be delighted to get them out of their
hair for a few months at a time.

Your upbringing is such that you are mixing with all different
types of people. In pre-prep school, you would mix with village
children and others, a complete mix of children, and of course
children don't really know anything about class at that age. If
you have one exceptionally wealthy person who lives in the big
house on the hill, then the parents of other children would
probably be talking and saying: his parents live up there, he
doesn't have any worries. Maybe some of that filters through at
that age. But then, when you go up to prep school at the age of
eight, again you are all in the same sort of environment with the
same sort of children. I couldn't say that there was one particular
time when I said: well there are three classes.

Obviously class awareness is a subconscious realisation over a
period of time that you were born different from other people. You
were born luckier than most, and not as lucky as some. I think
the system is such that at the top end of the system, with the
upper-class, there is less class distinction than there is at the
bottom. In other words there is less said about it (even less
thought about it) than at the bottom end of the working class or
middle class.

It is a gradual awareness, and it is subconscious. I don't
remember a day when I suddenly thought that it was them and
us. Obviously one knew in the back of one's mind that to go to a
place like *Eton* costs money. Therefore either your parents had it
or they didn't. My parents didn't, in fact. A family trust from

Drumoland paid for my education. It cost money to go there, and supposedly one got a better education than at the state school.

Accent is a Label

One thing that sets you aside is the way you speak. You are labelled; everyone is labelled. If you are born in the East End of London you are a cockney, but even if I were born in the East End of London, if we had a house there, the fact that my parents spoke in a particular way and the fact that children at the school spoke in a particular way, I would still come out the way that I am, and that is something that you are labelled with for life. I find it quite difficult at times in Ireland; I am automatically assumed to be English because I speak with an English accent. But that is the product of the upper-class public schools system.

I mixed with kids in Chelsea, and before with village children. That is the advantage of youth, you are innocent until you are corrupted by the grown-ups. When you are young you can mix with anyone without any problems, but the older you get (and as you get further into the system) you tend to conform with that system, and naturally your friends tend to conform with the system because it is a group. If I had a group of friends in my teens who were similar to me, and I introduced one of the street kids, he would be a fish out of water. There would not be an easy mix. Not that there would be any antagonism shown. Again I think that is the good thing about the system: you learn to get on with everyone, to deal with people. I had come to that from my army life. You relate to people working with you, to people under you, that sort of thing.

Holidays at Dromoland

I used to come over to Dromoland every summer on holidays. I had lots of friends, adult friends there that I got on very well with. They were working on a farm or living in the village. People like that, who you got to know and became very friendly with.

And still I am very friendly. Relationships were very easy, warm relationships. I never felt in Ireland any antagonism at all towards me in my adolescent years from anyone, and I don't think people felt they had to be nice to me because I was "the Lord". I think that it was just genuine friendships, and the Irish are much easier mixing with people. We don't have this stigma attached to the classes in Ireland as much as they do in England. Obviously there is some.

Nobody explained class in England. It was tradition more than anything else, particularly in my family's case, the history of the family, going so far back, and the type of upbringing we always had. It was tradition, and it was never a discussion that it was better than another system, it was just something that you were born into. You were brought up in that manner automatically.

Begininng with Brian Boru

I am a direct descendant of Brian Boru, the king of Ireland who died in 1014. After that kings of Ireland on and off, kings of Munster, kings of Thomond until 1543 when Murrough, who was the fifty-seventh king of Thomond submitted to King Henry VIII and became the Earl of Glen and Baron Inchiquin. That barony is the one which survived. So you might say that my family have been aristocratic since the time of Brian Boru. Therefore it is sort of inbred if you like. It is quite a history and tradition to have behind one. We then remained the same type of family and ever since then, by fighting on the right side at the right time — and sitting on the fence at the right time — we survived through Irish history. But we have done so at a cost over the years. In order to survive the time of King Henry VIII we had to submit to the King and forego our own kingdoms and lands. He granted the lands back again, and this has given me titles. Some Irish to-day think this was a sell-out, but we are still here. We have survived. We are not in Portugal, we are not in Spain, and we have played an active part in Irish history in those times, on and off. We have had some good and bad members of the family, a tremendous history, and the same type of land-owning family through the ages up until to-day.

Keeping it Together

It hasn't fallen apart. During the Cromwellian times, my name-sake, Conor O' Brien, was killed by Cromwell. His wife, Máire Rua, the red Mary, saved the family's estates by marrying one of Cromwell's officers. I wouldn't be living in Dromoland to-day if she hadn't done that. A book could be written on her. She was quite a colorful character. So I say: luck and a great many other things have enabled us to survive until to-day with some of our inheritance intact. We still have part of Dromoland estate, and of course all the history that goes with it.

More recent history pertains to the downfall of the landed classes of Ireland. I suppose that started in the 1880's with the land acts, when the income to the landlords disappeared, although their lifestyles didn't always change. To maintain a place like Dromoland costs money, so that was the start of the major financial problems of the family. If you go through the Civil War and the 1916 Uprising, the First World War, the Depression of the thirties, the Second World War, the inland revenue in the 20th century — all that brought about the difficulties of the land-owning families. It was a struggle, and there is no guarantee that anyone will succeed. Many families have lost everything they had and many families that were in positions of wealth and strength or whatever are now totally impoverished. In some cases living extremely hard lives on the bread line. We are lucky, so far we have survived. But we are not out of the snare yet. The tax man is still there and I still have to pay fifty percent of the value of the place which we inherited.

The idea of the trust was to keep a place like that together, to stop any irresponsible young person from gambling it or wasting it. Generally trustees were appointed to respect it. They are experienced people who make the decisions on how the money should be spent and what should be done. But in many cases the trust was set up two or three generations ago and no longer applied to the modern day circumstances. For example, questions of capital acquisitions tax which are extremely restrictive.

Getting Ulcers

As head of the family and head of the O'Brien's, and by tradition and upbringing, I have a position of responsibility and I don't want to be the one to fail in that, to lose everything or to sell out or to go abroad or to give up the ghost or suddenly go off the rails and do stupid things. That is again what it comes back to: one's upbringing, the way you were brought up and the responsibility you feel you have which grows on you through your adolescent years. As you get older, the responsibility sort of means more to you.

It is no lightweight responsibility, it is an ulcer I tell you. People automatically think he has got a title, he was born with a silver spoon in his mouth, he is very wealthy, he lives in a big house. It is not true. I mean it is not my house. It belongs to the trust. I am what you call a tenant. Okay I have the use of it, but no guarantee that it will survive. I had to sell some of the land to pay the capital acquisition tax on just under seven hundred acres of land, which is a huge amount although it is a small amount when you consider what we had before.

All of those sort of things you have to think about and worry about and make provisions for. So it is a big responsibility.

The ball is in my court. That is why the sort of upbringing I had is one which is sort of proven, if you like, over many generations. It has been shown that it works, that you are equipped both mentally and psychologically and historically and everything else to be able to deal with these sort of problems.

Travelling the World

I have travelled all over the world. I have really spent very little time in Europe, only really in my adolescent years in the U.K. Then, when I joined the army, I was abroad until I came to Ireland in eighty-two, and I have been in Ireland since then. I have friends all over the world, particularly in the Far East, where I lived in Hong Kong for nine years. I have four circles of friends: I have old school friends; I have army friends; I have Hong Kong friends; and I have Ireland friends. In many cases those four circles synergise to each other, some of them know each other, some of them maybe belong to the same circle. Most of them are the same sort of people. I have made a lot of friends whom I keep in contact with, and I travel quite a bit.

I think as you get older you broaden your net. In school you are in a circle and you mix with certain people. When I left school, and went into the army, I was with the same sort of people, although one comes into another relationship with one's soldiers, which is also something very special. The army officers have had a similar sort of upbringing. So in my case it wasn't really until after I left the army that I really broadened considerably my circle of friends, mainly through business. I have friends in all classes, principally upper/middle-class, but the older you get the wider the friendship net, the more easier it is to mix with everyone.

Handling the Soldiers

With your soldiers you have a very special relationship. There you have got the classic example of the upper-class working hand-in-hand with the lower-class or the working-class/lower class — whatever you want to call them. When the chips are down, what matters is that your soldiers do as you say and follow you to the ends of the earth. If you say jump over a cliff, they jump over a cliff. That is an exaggeration, of course. That is a very special relationship to develop. Soldiers, now I am talking about the rank and file, I am not talking about non-commissioned officers, I am talking about troopers, privates. In the British army, they tended to be the rough end of the working classes, petty criminals and people who don't fit in, people who find it difficult, who just need the discipline. You would think that you have got such opposites there that they shouldn't work. How could you mix a rough working-class type with an upper-class person and get a unit that works? It is something to do with respect and leadership. Its leading by example. Again I think part of it, from an officer's point of view, is one's upbringing, one's ability to mix. You've no chips on your shoulder, just the ability to get on with people. And of course your job is to manage people, management is what it is all about. So that is a very special relationship, which is a good example of how two opposites can work extremely well together. They might be held together slightly by discipline, but you do get very close when you are living in your tank for three months with three soldiers. You have to get on with them, and yet the respect is still there. You don't call them by their Christian names, and yet there is a general understanding and familiarity amongst you. They know how far they can go, and you know how far you can go. And you build the relationship on that. It is extraordinary. Again the other part of it is that it is built on tradition. The regimental tradition, as far as the British army is concerned. It is an amazing friendship actually, and I still keep in touch with some of my Irish regiment's soldiers.

I think it is one thing which we missed out on badly in Ireland. If we could have taken on the traditions of the old Irish regiment. I don't mean the English/Irish but the Irish regiments when we became a republic. I think we should have taken all those traditions on board and have Clare's Dragoons as opposed to the twenty-first battalion which has no identity, no history. We all have Irish history behind us, fighting for Ireland and not fighting for England, and it has all gone to waste. Perhaps it is considered too much like the English system. I don't know. But I think it is a pity.

A relationship with the opposite end of the scale can work very well. It probably wouldn't work so well in the middle end of the scale. If all your soldiers were middle-class, you probably would have many more problems. But traditionally the two ends, they work very well.

Business is the same. I mean if you want to get on in business, you have got to get on with people. If I went in with a pompous attitude, I wouldn't get anywhere. You can't change who you are or what you are, and people make up their own minds about the people they are dealing with. One of the things perhaps in favour of some of the upper-classes is that, generally speaking, they are fairly straight. I say "generally speaking" because you get people who are crooked, and it is a question of knowing the motivation in business. Whatever your business is, you are doing it to your mutual benefit, so you have to get on. I have never found any problems in business at all.

No Standing on Ceremony

In rural areas I am still treated, if you like, in the old school way. Particularly by the older folk around Dromoland. They will call you "your lordship" which not many people do now. That is the tradition. Yet at the same time I am Conor O'Brien to a lot of people and particularly the younger people, I don't stand on any ceremony and I am Conor O' Brien to most people. Being "your Lordship", that is difficult. I find it difficult to adjust to that because having lived all my life as Conor O' Brien, made my own way in life and I did my own thing. Then, inheriting from my uncle, I came back to Ireland and overnight I become supposedly a different person with a different name. It is not a name it is a title. That has been difficult to adjust to. And again I think the education has helped me in that. The way I have been educated has enabled me to know when to be informal. and when to accept the respect from the older people. That is something which one's upbringing teaches you. But I will never fully adjust to it. I mean as far as most of the Irish are concerned, I am English. And I have an English title, as far as the Irish are concerned. Although the English think me Irish, so I can't sit in the House of Lords. So I am in the middle. I was born with a bit of a millstone around my neck. You have just got to adjust to it somehow. There is nothing you can do about it.

The New Generation

My children's generation will probably be the first generation which will be considered as Irish, and even they will have difficulties because they will be educated in Ireland. They will speak with an Irish accent. They are the ones who will be ragged at school because of who their parents are. They will go to the local school initially, but then possibly they will go to boarding school, maybe when they are twelve or thirteen or something like that. And it won't be an English school; it will be an Irish school. But they will be brought up with the same principles and the same traditions and the same ideas and morals and everything that I and my wife have had to live.

Nineteen Irish Chiefs

Mine is actually an Irish heritage, but it depends how you are writing, because as far as the Irish are concerned it is English, and as far as the English are concerned it is Irish. My title is of Irish heritage because it was created before the Act of Union. It is one of those strange areas. I am the only one to hold an Irish heritage and an Irish Chieftaincy. There are now nineteen Irish chiefs. In fact we met recently for the first time, we had a historic meeting of seventeen. I think it was the first meeting of the chiefs since the Battle of Kinsale, and we went to "Aras an Uchtarain" and met President Robinson, then we formed the standing council of Irish Chiefs which is set up really to promote cultural areas in Ireland, historical areas. Some people would say you shouldn't be there or shouldn't be recognised. I mean the Irish Government recognises the Irish Chiefs as a matter of courtesy and as the legal representatives of the old Gaelic families, the ones that have proved their claim by documentary evidence. We are certainly all very proud to be who we are, to form this Council, and we hope that we can play some part in the future of Ireland. We are not a political organisation, we have no pretensions of taking over the country again or anything like that, but we are all extremely proud of our ancestors and their history.

The new Taoiseach has nothing to worry about from us, well unless he does things that we don't totally agree with, I mean we might have a say then.

History of the Castle

I think obviously one is proudest of one's family tradition and heritage and the parts of history that the O'Briens have played from Brian Boru down. We have Smith O'Brien, who led the uprising in 1848. I am proud that we have managed to survive through a very turbulent six or seven hundred years. By that I mean that, as head of the O'Briens and head of the main branch of the O'Brien family, my branch and family have survived through that. The areas that one would want to forget or, one wouldn't play up as much would be the fact that we were forced into submission in the mid-fifteen hundreds, against our will. The only alternative was to refuse to submit and lose everything and disappear into the hills and play no future part in the history of Ireland. Or leave the country and go to Spain or Portugal or France or something.

We have had O'Briens like Murrough the Burner, a famous general who burned the rock of Cashel, apparently trying to get the bishop. He didn't get the bishop but burned a number of priests and hence got the nick name of Murrough the Burner. His body was thrown in the Shannon, and the next day he was buried at St Mary's. I think he is harshly judged by history. I think you have to look at the times. They were pretty barbaric on all sides. You held no quarter for your enemy, you couldn't surrender. He is portrayed as a black sheep of the family, but he was a fine general and did a lot of very good things for Ireland as well. I am also proud of Máire, who saved the family estates by marrying one of Cromwell's officers after her husband was killed.

A Proud Tradition

I am proud that we have got through the whole period of Irish independence in becoming a Republic which were difficult times for us because we were very much viewed as anglicised Irish. Yes, we were anglicised, but so were most of the Irish. People say so much about the submissions and we shouldn't have submitted to Henry VIII and we shouldn't have learnt English. But everyone in the country speaks English, so then everyone is anglicised. But we got through that period, Dromoland survived during the Troubles. The IRA sent down two petrol barrels to burn it, but the local branch of the IRA put a stop to it as we were considered good landlords. We employed most of the locals, so if they burned down the house, then the employment would go as well. But I think basically we were considered good landlords.

We have survived against the Inland Revenue so far, with great difficulty. We are still there and we intend to stay there; and there is a lot to do. I am involved particularly in the tourism and leisure side. Dromoland Castle is now a hotel, employing a lot of people. The estate, the part of the estate which I have is very much a sporting estate, We have pheasant shoots which employ twenty or thirty people at times, so there is a lot going on there and the emphasis has changed. But we are still there.

Aristocracy

The roll of aristocracy depends on which country you are looking at. I think in the U.K. it still plays an important part, the House of Lords is seen now (particularly since it has been televised) as an effective upper house. And the majority of peers who sit in the House of Lords actually work reasonably hard and do a good job. Of the hereditary peers, there are some who work hard and some who don't.

The aristocracy is connected with very fine buildings and properties which are open to the public as museums. In many cases they are owned by the National Trust. This is a credit to those families that have the will and the incentive to try and keep the place together, rather than letting it get broken up, as has happened in Ireland sadly.

Ireland is a difficult question. There isn't a place for the aristocrat in Ireland as such. The Irish don't want him. There aren't as many in Ireland, and they don't play the same sort of part in Ireland, so it is a difficult question in Ireland. Mind you, when you get a royal wedding on television, the streets would be emptied. So there is an interest. But I don't think there is a future, as such, for aristocracy in Ireland. We are a Republic, we as chiefs are recognised by courtesy not by right, and I don't see that changing. However I think as chiefs we do have a role to play in modern Ireland and the future of Ireland and that is what we are discussing and developing at the moment with the standing Council of the Chiefs.

Not a Politcal Role

There is no political role for the aristocrat. However, in the case of someone like Henry Mount Charles, if he wants to go into politics (which he was considering at one stage) and he is a good politician then he should be judged on his politics rather than on his title, and be given the chance to do that. But I somehow think that he would be up against a tremendous stigma because of his title. It is very difficult for a titled person in Ireland to hold any form of public office.

The constitution doesn't allow for any titles of honour or position or anything like that. There is no recognition as such. I suppose that is one of the reasons in dealing with the politicians there is always a feeling that you're representing the lot we got out, fought so long to get out. But I have never felt animosity from any politician that I deal with, and I deal with quite a lot of them.

To be an aristocrat in Ireland is a bit of a millstone. But it does get you a good seat in a restaurant. It gets you through the switchboard quicker than most, and it can be useful sometimes from a corporate side if you want to have a title on the board. There are some advantages. But behind it all lurks the revenue people. Survival is difficult, or rather, hanging onto what is left is difficult. I know some people say we shouldn't have it in the first place, but on the other hand I would say you can gladly have it — and all the problems that go with it.

Saving the Estate

If I sold up, I would still have to work. Having sold the land and everything and paid all the duties and everything else, there would probably be enough to live comfortably. But I would still have to work, still have to earn a living. I think one of the reasons I am working in Dublin now three or four days a week is because there was no money in farming, farming is not going to save the estate. The only way we will save the estate is making some money elsewhere and putting it into the estate. Anyway, I have worked all of my life, and I would never be a person who would go off and live a leisured existence.

There were times in the mid-eighties, when I really felt that I had bashed my head against a brick wall for long enough, that if things didn't begin to improve or look better that I would give it up. But I suppose secretly I have always felt that I would never do that.

If confiscated, I would fight against it obviously. But if it were taken away, well then it is taken away. It has happened in many countries before and people have survived and carried on their lives. The same would happen to me. I would carry on with my life.

The responsibilities and things would have been taken off my shoulders, although one still has to work. Because of one's upbringing and tradition, one would find it very difficult to lose it all, or be in the chair when it was taken away, or fell, or whatever. I think it would have more of an effect psychologically than anything else.

NOEL BROWNE

Manning the Barricades

Born in 1915, Noel Browne's childhood was disrupted by the deaths of his father and an infant sister of TB, before his already ill mother moved the family to England. Soon his mother, a brother and two more sisters had died of TB, which he himself was to contract in 1940. Kindly interventions and scholarship allowed him to be educated and become a doctor. In 1948 he was appointed Minister for Health on his first day in the Dail. He strove vigorously to eliminate TB and undertook a massive hospital building programme, however his Ministerial career floundered in 1951 when he tried to introduce the Mother and Child Scheme. Disagreement within Clann na Poblachta over the issue led to his resignation and a subsequent general election. He remained active in politics as a TD and Senator until 1982, being seen for many years as a sole voice for independent, intellectual and socialist politics. His autobiography was a huge best-seller in 1986. He now lives in a remote cottage in Connemara with his wife Phyllis and they have recently celebrated their 50th wedding anniversary.

My parents were from East Galway, from a largely rural background. My mother and father were literate, but not educated in any kind of sense at all. My mother seemed to be the more literate of the two of them. She had an extraordinary fund of aphorisms, for a person who probably didn't have any education beyond, say, nine or ten years — sayings which I still keep with me. My father was able to write and he worked as an inspector for the National Society for Prevention of Cruelty to Children, having to do reports and go to courts and all that sort of thing. I can't remember seeing books in the house except my own books, the books I liked. I don't think my parents were unhappy; I don't think they knew any better. At that time the level of illiteracy was very high, and their expectations of life were very modest. They were a happy pair, and they were deeply in love.

Basic Diet of Potatoes

My background was varied, sort of working-class — middle-working-class. Our first home was in Waterford, where I was born, then we moved to Derry. In the beginning it was pretty primitive and basic, because in Derry my father was working in a shirt factory, doing piece work and that was at the level of slum life. We left Derry then and went to live in Athlone. There my father's job was as an inspector in the NSPCC and I think he was quite happy with his job. There was a lot of poverty at that time; large families with too many children. His job was to go around and try to improve the welfare of these children. Many were sent to industrial schools, a dreadful solution to a dreadful problem, but that was the way things were. It was better paid — £11.00 a fortnight. It seems tiny now but we had three meals a day, although it was a basic diet of potatoes and certainly no luxuries at all. I use to do the milk rounds in a donkey and cart for Mr Molloy. I think the wife of Mr Molloy had a great deal of sympathy for my mother, with so many mouths to feed, and she always used to give me a big can of milk.

My father died of TB when I was nine or ten years of age. Up until that time I knew nothing else. I knew no other life. I had the usual life of a young boy growing up in rural Ireland. I read a lot and there were the usual games in the street, hop scotch and all the usual tops and hoops and things like that. It was a pleasant life. I had no sense of grievance at all because I didn't know there was any other kind of life, and I was quite happy.

Chanting in Athlone

At one stage I think my parents hoped I would go to Mungret and become a priest. That was the usual thing. But the death of my father stopped everything. I was going to the Christian Brothers school in Athlone. I don't think I could have gone to the secondary school in Athlone even though it was the Marist Brothers and was only a small fee. I doubt if my father could have paid that small fee.

It was such a strange school, because we had only a little bit of serious teaching. Our main teacher, Brother John, taught us how to sing Gregorian chant. He was mad about it and we stood on the desks all day and we sang and sang and sang. That is all I remember of school in Athlone. Then we moved on. After my father's death, we went to Ballinrobe, and then things changed a great deal.

I got approval by being a good boy. I don't recall ever being chastised or anything, except on one occasion when I stayed outside the door during the First Holy Communion at school. The Marist Brothers used to give a big breakfast and I was around at the time and the teacher Mr Hanly, a nice man, invited me into the breakfast. When I got home my mother was terribly upset because she felt that people might think I was hungry and she being a proud country girl, felt very angry about that. She thought I had begged the breakfast, which I hadn't. She tried to beat me, poor pet, but because of course she had never done that before in her life, she got a stick that wasn't very strong. We were all very fond of her, she was a gentle mother and I don't think anybody had to raise their voice to get listened to. We did what we were told. My family were very undemonstrative. My mother would smile at you, and that was about all you could expect. There was no cuddling or kissing or anything like that, but you knew that she was glad you were there and that you were alright. So we had a very uncontentious family life. I often used to go off with a family who had a farm outside of Athlone and I spent most of my time there. I used to drive the donkey and cart home and there was a little girl there called Maura, and Maura and I used to have a lovely time around the country. I spent my time more with girls than boys, and we had a country children's life. I would come home to do the little homework I had, and then go to bed.

Athlone was a beautiful place at the time, and we would all go off in our different directions. Mother had this extraordinary practice — at about 5 o'clock she would stand at the edge of the door which opened out onto the main street in Athlone, and she would whistle in a particular way, like calling a sheep dog or something, and we would all troop back from wherever we were in Athlone. A lot of our playing was down by the river which was not very far, about five or six hundred yards away, and when we heard her whistle we knew it was time to come back for tea.

I think that the best things about growing up in a poor rural background was the peace and the security that come from the sense that my parents were always there, the feeling of 'den' when you got in out of the weather, or the school or whatever it might be, and you got back home to the pleasant feeling of being out of the war zone. That sense of security stemmed largely from my mother.

We had neighbours called Bracken, a bigger, a more wealthy family, by our standards. When our mother was in bed giving birth to another child, Mrs Bracken would become our surrogate mother. She was a gentle, soft-spoken women, endlessly smiling and always anxious and available to help. Mrs Bracken was a big powerful woman, and always wore a big old canvas apron around her capacious middle.

The Discreet Island

The limitations of my background are, I think, peculiar to our society. It is what I recently described as our idea of amoral familism. The family was an island within the community, made up of inlaws, and aunties and uncles and so on. It was a discreet unit within a community in which there was nothing else except discreet units, and I suppose the only sense of unity in the community would be the sense of the parish, although I was not conscious of that at the time. I don't know if my mother or father knew that there was such a thing as a parish either. We had little contact with the clerics, they didn't take any interest in us; of course we had just come into Athlone. I don't know whether it was because we were considered newcomers or outsiders, but with the exception of the Brackens next door, we had no other source of support.

There is this isolation, an active isolation to my mind, in our culture, within the Irish ethos of the individual family in society. There may be these occasional support units outside the individual family, such as another family or inlaws, but it doesn't go any further than that. This became infinitely more obvious later on when we moved to Ballinrobe. There was this very selective concern for fellow human beings in society. It didn't go beyond the immediate family, or a select group of families in the near neighbourhood. We never had any contact with our neighbours on our right hand side at all. They were teachers, a bit above us; and across the road from us were the Duffys, rather above us again, so we had no contact except playing with the children. We were very rigidly encapsulated within our own family. You were educated into this: that family is your concern, and outside that you didn't care.

Poverty is a Big Stick

Other limitations were the products of poverty: the lack of choice in relation to education, the standard of living, medical facilities, holidays, reading, music. I was very fond of music, but I could never have been able to afford to become a musician. Nobody could afford it. It was a subsistence existence, with the main priority being to survive, that was about all. Very humiliating, very demoralising, and the more you look back at it, the worse it becomes. Poverty is a sort of big stick that is used to maintain the structure of society by upholding a particular attitude to society. Having money or not having it, became the dynamic for avarice, greed and selfishness as I later saw.

In childhood I had contact with a number of people better off than my family. The Begley's on the left were builders, and although they had quite a big yard, we had little contact with them. Across the road the Duffys, higher up the ladder, used to entertain all the officers from Athlone Barracks at the time. We used to play with the Duffy children, but we knew we were below them in social status. They had this big yard in which we played all sorts of games and listened to music on an old music box. Then there were the Molloys, who were substantial farmers. They were above us also, as they had a biggish house and a biggish farm outside of Athlone. So we were different from those two.

I knew all three lives were different to ours. We lived in a small over-crowded house. We had only three bedrooms, and there were nine or ten of us, while they had spacious homes and grounds. But I didn't envy them. I was happy in myself, and in my home, and in my relationships within the family. I didn't feel that I had been seriously deprived in any way, at least not that I can remember. There was nothing I particularly admired about better-off people, not at that stage; later on, in Ballinrobe, yes. That was simply because there we were obviously so grossly deprived that there was an element of suffering in it, which was dramatically different to Athlone. In Athlone, I had a pleasant, secure home in which I had two loving parents. We had the ordinary childish squabbles and so on, but we had a happy time. I would say I was quite happy with my lot. In Ballinrobe, every thing changed. We went down. Even though we were low on the social scale in Athlone, in Ballinrobe we went lower still.

In Ballinrobe

We had no running water, which was a severe blow — the awful business of the dry toilet. I had a brother who was a little hunch back. He had TB, and even when he was in his thirties, he was only about three-and-a-half feet high. He had this awful hump and a hairlip; he was a cripple. That meant that, as the only other boy I became the head of the family, and from then on I began to see that everything was quite different for people with money. I had to go to the river to bring back buckets of water, which was dreadful. At least in Athlone we had running water, cold running water. Now I had the appalling job of emptying buckets of what they used to call night soil. It was terrible. As a youngster I was hardly able to lift the bucket. Naturally I would put it off, and the longer I put it off the worse it became. It was a very dreadful ordeal.

Then my mother became ill or rather she got worse. She had TB and must have also had a kidney disease, because she was in great pain and would lie on the sofa moaning. Everything changed then. We became the parents in the family, looking after her. And we were happy to do it as long as we could. We did not know that she had no money. She had one hundred pounds for the whole lot of us; no widow's or orphan pensions, no money coming into the house. She knew the money was going to run out. That would mean each of us would end up in those terrible industrial schools, like the ones my father used to send children to who were deprived. She had all these signs of advanced tuberculosis and that lasted for a year or maybe two years. But during that time everything changed. The way you saw people changed! We had no food really. Poor Joedy, my hunchback brother, had to go to work in the grocery shop. He used to ride the messenger-boy bicycle. For that he got little or nothing, but he also got the bits and pieces from the bacon machine, so that was our Sunday dinner.

Everything had collapsed as soon as we went to Ballinrobe. Now I knew the penalty of poverty. I went to school in the Christian Brothers, then quite a different school, with a lot of hard work to be done. I always did well in school, I never had any problems in any school I was ever in, I never got into trouble, except once in Beaumont. But in Ballinrobe it was a terrifying experience watching the other boys getting beaten. A horrible, terrible thing! I used to sit up the front of the class and the Brother would beat them mercilessly.

The Envy of Leather Boots

Envy came into my mind then. I had a good friend, Tommy Breath, who was the son of a wealthy draper. I envied Tommy, his clothes. For instance, we wore leather boots with steal toe capping and all that, and Tommy had lovely leather boots laced up with criss-cross things you know and knickerbocker trousers and lovely woollen socks. We had none of those things. And then there were the big houses with their own apple trees. We had none of that kind of thing, and it was hard not to feel envious.

I saw a lot of poverty, a lot of poor people, poorer than us even, many of them dying. Looking back now, a lot of them obviously had TB. You watched them wasting away and you wondered what was wrong with them. Then eventually they would disappear and you would know they had died.

I think a lot of the seeds of my discontent probably had their origins in Ballinrobe, watching my mother die and not being able to afford a doctor. We just had to sit around her there while she was crying. She was a beautiful woman and we hated seeing her crying, and that really emphasised the horror of poverty and the infiniteness of poverty.

The Will of God

My mother's view of why there are 'haves and have nots' was very simply that it was the Will of God and His Holy Mother, and we mustn't complain because this is the way things are, that the world is divided up between wealthy people and the others and there is no remedy for it. You accept it and if you are fortunate you will go up to Heaven when you die and you will be happy forever after. I never asked any questions about why it was like this. I lived in great fear, great distress because of the humiliation of my life and it was utterly different to Athlone altogether. I saw a lot of people, a lot of widows who had children and they found it hard to make ends meet. You could see from their pallor and their clothes that they were cold and hungry. We weren't happy children like we were in Athlone. Everything changed very much in Ballinrobe.

My mother was approaching death from advanced tuberculosis, and the hundred pounds was running out. She knew if that happened we would be sent off to reform or industrial school. Eileen my eldest sister, had got a job in a holiday school where children of people who were out in the Colonies stayed outside of term time. British people used to send their children there, ones who couldn't bring their children out to the Far East, so they sent them to these holiday schools.

My mother decided she couldn't go on any longer. I remember walking along the street home from school and seeing a notice announcing the Browne family's auction. Everything was to be sold. Once that was done, my mother bought tickets to London. She then endured this extraordinary journey, suffering from terminal TB. She brought us down to Kingstown, (it was Dun Laoghaire then I suppose), and we crossed over, catching the train to London where we stayed with some people Eileen knew in a place called Heron Hill. I remember it very well, it's kind of burnt into my consciousness. We weren't in that house more than a couple of days when my mother finally collapsed and the last thing I remember was when she was out in the hallway and we were each of us asked to go out and bid farewell and kiss her on the forehead. She then went off and died and she was buried in a pauper's grave.

Orphan Amongst the Wealthy

The sister of the proprietors of the holiday school took me into St Anthony's, a very exclusive prep school for wealthy young Catholic boys. Many of them were from abroad, as there was not an awful lot of wealthy Catholic families in England. A lot were the children of wealthy families, ambassador's children from Latin America, Chile or Argentina, Peru, the Middle East, France and even a few wealthy Irish Catholic (oddly enough, Daly from

Ballinrobe). It was all very cosmopolitan, and a lovely little school really. I suddenly found myself far from the total deprivation, degradation and humiliation of life in Ballinrobe, in superb surroundings, playing fields and swimming pools, small classes and exotic foods.

After St Anthony's I went to Beaumont College in England, where I stayed for three or four years. I had no problem with academic subjects. I became one of the heads or captains of the place. I played in all the teams; games were very important in England. I got all my exams; School Certificate was the important exam, rather like the Leaving Certificate here.

At that stage the lady died, the holiday school closed and I had a hectic time then, with no home. I lived with all sorts of people, but mostly very wealthy people, aristocratic castles. But also in working-class homes. All sorts of places.

Adopted Family

Eileen had contracted TB too, and she was in hospital. That was the beginning of a great insecurity which haunts me still really, a sort of nightmare business, being on my own and, nobody knowing me, no ties, no links. People passing me by, not taking any interest in me, unable to catch a bus home, unable to get to wherever I wanted to and not knowing where I wanted to go anyway. Being in Beaumont I had to stay in the school when holidays came, as I had nowhere to go, and all my friends were heading off to their various homes, so I was left with the big empty echoing corridors. However one boy, Neville Chance, asked if I wanted to go to Dublin to stay with him and his family. Lady Chance was the second wife of Sir Arthur Chance, who had a very large family, two families, one older than the other. But at the end of my holiday I had nowhere to go back to in England because by then Eileen was in Italy. A priest in Soho, had managed to get her out to a villa for her health. The Chance family knew that I was helpless, penniless and homeless, and the senior Chance brothers got together and asked me if I would like to go to Trinity.

I was delighted and said yes. I could not believe my luck, as it was beyond my wildest hopes and dreams that I would ever be anything. So I remained living with Lady Chance in her beautiful large houses. I never had any trouble at Trinity, and got all my exams, but unfortunately got TB myself just when I was doing my finals.

In both St Anthony's and Beaumont College there were extremely wealthy, privileged people, with beautiful homes, but none of them had the fears that I had. They didn't know these things existed, that you couldn't become anything that you wanted to be. Most of them went off to the army, the artillery, gunners and engineers, and some of them went to Dartmouth, the Naval College, to become naval officers. Everybody was very much the officer class, destined to be the leaders of society and they had plenty of money to attain anything that they wished. If they wanted to be doctors or lawyers or architects, it was only really a matter of saying that is what I want to be, and they could be it. They may not have been conscious of any other life. The whole indoctrination of the class system was that life is as it is and there is nothing that you can do to change it, and the poor will always be with us. That is readily accepted. The alternative is going out there into the streets, mounting barricades and saying that I don't agree that there should be poor people in the gutter and bagmen and bagwomen sleeping rough. You say I don't agree with that, I want to change society and make it otherwise. I want to give everyone the opportunities I have. It is very rare you will get anybody who will turn away from Oxford, Cambridge or any of the universities on that basis. The whole force of the educational system is about maintaining the class system and the futility of change. You can't right the wrongs by yourself, so why rock the boat?

Rejecting the System

I think the divisions were very rigidly maintained and the defence mechanisms and the barriers were consciously and carefully defined between classes. They were there because they deserve to be there and we are here because we deserve to be here. I never really heard any kind of serious dissention from school-teachers etc. The last lecture we had from the rector of Beaumont was that we were the leaders of society and we were to take our places with dignity, and so on but there was no question of changing the class structure of society or interfering with it in any way.

I suppose I assimilated very quickly into everything with little or no difficulty. It was pleasant, and I took it as part of the way life was. It was only later on, when I had to make choices about whether I would go on and use my profession to make an awful lot of money, that I made the deliberate choice not to, that I did not agree with what I saw. I could not suffocate my conscience with the anodynes of the world that way, and I could not be happy in my own life while I saw so much unhappiness around.

My family were all scattered over different places, and although we would meet in the holidays from school, we ceased to be a family. I was simply an individual, a homeless individual. My life went on and I had holidays with different families, but I never felt tempted to embrace their lifestyle. I did all the point to point with the hunters, sailing, yachting, lovely cars, everything you could imagine. I saw all that wealth could buy but I knew that would never appeal to me. I knew that on account of my family, my background, I shouldn't be there at all.

Doctor for a Reason

The deaths in my family facilitated my journey through medical school. This has always offended me as a human being, this 'whimsical' nature of life for everybody not just me. I have such a regard for human beings, the suffering that many have to endure through no fault of their own is very upsetting to watch. And naturally it happened in my own family. Eileen died in isolation in Italy and then Joedy my poor little brother died, in terrible circumstances. You couldn't be unmarked by that. You would have to be terribly cold-blooded not to be deeply marked by it. And I think that certainly happened as far as I was concerned. The fact that I was so helpless, penniless, homeless was the reason why the Chance family said they would help me, and it was the way to my eventually becoming a doctor. As you know, as a doctor you can have a wonderful life but I didn't choose it for that. I was too scarred, I think, by my life experiences to conceive of getting any pleasure out of career advancement. Watching what was going on, I thought I could do something.

Fortunately, I met this marvellous girl, all those years ago. And we got married. Phyllis has a similar background, upper-middle/lower-middle class, Church of Ireland family. I certainly have been marked, deeply marked by my life experience and I'm not sorry. I'm very happy if there is anything that I can do to mitigate people's suffering. But the fascinating thing is that unlike every other member of our respective families, she and I are the only ones to feel this way.

I never liked politics; politics is so futile. At one stage I wanted to go back into medicine with the intention of getting involved in the study of genetics. I was interested in the whole debate about nature, nurture and the psycho-sexual development of people in the early years of their lives, and to the extent that the genetic component of one's psyche, (the joker in the pack so to speak), determines our final persona which comes out of our life experience.

"Damn your Charity...."

Of course it was wonderful that the Chance family were there at the time and that they chose to make that decision to help me. But I can't forget my brother Joedy. I can't forget mother and Eileen and my father. I cannot ignore the fact that it was completely accidental, that it needn't have happened. And of course, as a politician, my claim has always been it shouldn't have happened, there was no necessity for this kind of gratuitous charity. The workers who marched down to London in the hunger marches of the thirties had a banner which I always think says every thing. It said 'Damn your charity, we want justice'. I was interested in this objective sense of justice. I wanted to concern myself with the accidents which bedevil the lives of other people, of feeling you have a responsibility to try to help them. Society should be so arranged that the accidental nature of life is taken into consideration. For me, it was an extraordinary tragic accident that poverty took my parents from me so early in life, and my good fortune that made it possible for me to make whatever contribution that I have made to alleviate the suffering of people by promoting particular political points throughout my life. It is the blatant dismissal of these 'accidents' that angers me very much. I could be working on the roads, or as a binman, with every bit as much talent, but unable to express these talents because I was not born into a particular class. I think it is one of the great crimes of society that it allows this to happen. The idea that anybody would be needlessly squandered because of a defective institution is the greatest crime to my way of thinking, and why it is impossible for me to stand aside.

Politics for Change

It is very hard to generalise about what is obviously a complex subject. I think if you take all the classes, the peasant and the working class, the middle class and its graduations, and then the upper class, the motivation behind the dynamic which drives the individual to take an interest in society on the side of attempting to mitigate the inequalities, privilege, deprivation varies in each of them. For the peasant class, the motivation was usually the land. In my experience the pursuit of objective justice was very rare at that level, except for people like Michael Davitt. But the totally deprived individual in society is the peasant class and the idea of amoral familism is very highly developed in rural society. Lenin's idea is that the working class is the only revolutionary class. I tend to be rather cynical about that. I find it hard to believe that the workers are the fountainhead of all that's good, kind and generous and compassionate. I think that is an over-compensation, because of a sense of guilt. The working class motivation most of the time seems to me just as suspect as anyone's, because I have watched so many fall away from the pursuit of justice among the working class by members of the working class as soon as their personal needs are satisfied.

In the middle class, there is the existence of the sort of dilettante interest in suffering and poverty, the impoverished and the underprivileged. My feelings were always that it was not long-lasting. I saw very clear limitations to how the concern would last. It depended on the sacrifices needed to really change society, and that would more likely affect the middle class probably. They feel threatened by the prospect of moving down a class themselves and precious few were prepared to confront that possibility. As for the aristocracy, the very wealthy people, with the exceptions of Bertrand Russell and Tony Benn, I have seen little evidence of guilty feelings among most of them. My life was strange in that I crossed the divide and many of my early experiences were in yacht clubs and race meetings, point to points and expensive clubs of one kind or another. I have lived among wealthy people, and the rationalisation of the discrepancy between their lives and the lives of the vast majority of people in society worries very few of them.

"Pull up the Ladder, Jack..."

But I really couldn't say that I would be prepared to accept that the dynamic of poverty that drives so many people to protest and to revolutionary organisations is as wholesome as it claims. Often it is born out of a sense of envy of someone with better conditions, and when that difference is altered and remedied, the fact that there are others is ignored — "Pull up the ladder Jack, I'm alright" is a very prevalent attitude amongst all the classes.

At the same time, there are campaigners for social change within each level of the class structure, from say Davitt to Bertrand Russell and Tony Benn, who have a lasting persistent concern to the point of self-sacrifice, whether it be in financial or physical terms. I don't know which class I would look to more than another. Literacy comes into all this also and that is why I think you can exclude (shameful fact that it is) the peasant, because of the high level of illiteracy, the rural people (the peasants) possibly don't know that they are misled in to believing, like my mother and father, that the world can't be any other way. But even if they knew, I don't know that you would find any higher percentage of them manning the barricades, any more that you would in the Royal Irish Yacht Club. I remain very puzzled by it. It is a fascinating enigma.

Wounds on the Psyche

There is no doubt that my experience of loss as a child left me with ineradicable wounds, deep wounds, on my psyche, that I will bring to my grave. I must be a very gloomy person in many ways, as it seems to continue to pre-occupy my mind always. The only serious interest I have in life is trying to help to change society, to change the scale, the ugliness of it for so many people, and I think it stems from what I saw in my parents, two young people getting married and having too large a family and not enough money and getting a disease which is curable and preventable and dying when they were still young. It was a great crime. I can't say, that if I had been brought up from the beginning in a privileged house that I would never have seen the suffering. I can't imagine myself any different from the way I am.

Fanatical Concern for Life

Medicine wasn't my first choice. The Chances were a medical family and it seemed madly presumptuous of me to say what I would like to be and above all insanely presumptuous to say I would like to be a doctor. It was beyond my wildest dreams. I would have been happy with anything, well not happy with anything but at that stage there was simply nothing, I had no home, I hadn't a penny in my pocket. So therefore to be a doctor was a prize beyond price. Fortunately for me, emotionally it seems to have suited me very well. I derived great satisfaction from it, I loved the job, I loved the people, I always worked with poor people, I never worked for money, I always worked for a salary. That was all I wanted out of life. Even putting in a tree that has been torn out of the ground, putting it back in again and seeing it grow, a fanatical concern for life and respect for the organism of the living body, whether it is a spider in the bath or a human being. My great hero, I suppose in theatre and writing, is Sam Beckett, I have a rather sombre, gloomy view of life you see, and I see passing the time as a sort of an endurance test. As for the middle class, it is very difficult to blame them for surrounding themselves with protection against reality, the harshness of not having money; and poverty, particularly in our kind of society where the penalties of poverty are so harsh and so unfair and unjust. To me the middle class is really penned into a lifestyle which I suppose many of them feel ashamed of. But they are frightened into the pen by what they see outside, what they know is outside and what they see that other fellow human beings have to endure, the beggars and the bagmen and bagwomen and the children, all sleeping rough, the deprivation of love and the effect of deprivation of love in the evolution of the personality. I suppose it is true to say a thoughtful middle class person is a frightened person, frightened of the possibility of poverty. And that is rather humiliating. And then there are the hoops through which they have to jump so life becomes more and more like the life of a circus animal. The uniform of the striped suit, and the conventions, and the greed attitudes and patterns of social behaviour outside which you can't stray without criticism. I think it is a very stressful existence.

No More Panaceas

I remember not long ago talking to Eamonn Casey here and saying to him (after I had been in London, and saw mainly Irish youngsters sleeping in cardboard cities): why can't you go down to the church and preach a sermon and make them ashamed of the fact that these are our children and so on? He said they were sending out-reach curates to look after them. Always panaceas! Pat them on the head! Then the anodyne and the mad pursuit of deadening the inner voice. There are many ways of doing that open to the middle class.

In spite of what the middle class think, I think there is loss for them in the present organisation of life. I am possibly projecting my own discontent with that kind of approach to life. I basically can't understand how they can live side by side with all the inequities of our society, without being very uncomfortable. Looking at our admissions in a week at St. Loman's and the Eastern Health Board — I think eight out of ten people coming in are alcoholics, and they are from the middle class. Alcohol is the anodyne; or the valium effect of alcoholism is especially linked to the dreadful conformism of middle-class life; what is tolerated and what isn't, is unnatural. I think it is an unnatural existence, and the penalties are so frightening for the middle class (of not conforming) — even for myself and Phyllis. So few of our friends understand why I, a doctor, don't make a good living, have a big car and a big house and all those sort of things. They wonder why we don't do these things. And we feel that they must be very uncomfortable doing them.

In my view the best political direction for the middle classes is the development of community concern, community concern for every individual within that community. In Christian teaching, in the Gospels, there is an enormous amount of simple instruction on how one should live. The paradox for me is that this deeply religious country lives such a pagan existence. There is a contradiction between people's protestations and what they are prepared to accept — the divisions, the inequality, the privilege and the silence of the shepherd church about the obvious failure of people to live to the prescriptions of their religious teaching.